The Silver Grille

Memories and Recipes

New and Expanded Edition

Richard E. Karberg

with Judith Karberg and Jane Hazen

Published by
Cleveland Landmarks Press, Inc.
13610 Shaker Boulevard, Suite 503
Cleveland, Ohio 44120-1592
www.clevelandbook.com
(216) 658-4144

New and Expanded Edition
Copyright © 2002, Cleveland Landmarks Press, Inc.

ISBN–0-936760-18-4

LIBRARY OF CONGRESS CONTROL NUMBER– 2002092414

Designed by
Rusty Schneider
Moonlight Publishing
Hinckley, Ohio

Printed by Phillips Brothers
Springfield, Illinois

Dedication

To all the women and men of The Silver Grille,
who made dining there such a memorable experience,
and to the leadership of Forest City Enterprises
for bringing it back

Front Cover Photograph: The Silver Grille as it looked after renovation, May 3, 2002.
(Douglas Bardwell photo, courtesy of Forest City Enterprises)

Acknowledgments

Back in 1997 I knew I had to write about The Silver Grille and The Higbee Company department store at Public Square. That year I had the opportunity to tour the upper floors of the Higbee Building, which were then unused. Going upstairs in the building was like roaming through an ancient ruin. The rooms were dusty, but they unmistakably still reflected their one-time grandeur. The silent though intact Silver Grille stood as a monument to a bygone age. That visit compelled me to tell the story of that legendary place.

A chance conversation during a lunch break at the well-known White Elephant sale of the Cleveland Botanical Garden in November 1999 further cemented my commitment to the project. One of the other volunteers, Josie Gruden, told me that her cousin, Ann Zupancic, had managed The Silver Grille and had books of the restaurant's recipes. Discovering that those materials were available proved the breakthrough that allowed me to move forward with this project.

Shortly afterwards at the board meeting of the Cleveland Artists Foundation, I talked to Professor Gladys Haddad of Case Western Reserve University, who told me of a talk given by Jim McConnell, the last food service manager at Higbee's, who also had saved Silver Grille materials.

Ann Zupancic and Jim McConnell graciously allowed me access to their collections, as did Margaret Halterlein, the last manager of The Silver Grille, who also provided much material for this book.

I am also grateful to Robert Keller, Drew Rolik, and William Voegele of Forest City Enterprises, each of whom was generous with his time, resources, and patience; to Ken Jordan of Dillard's, who provided great assistance as well, and to Jerry W. Hoegner of the *Plain Dealer,* who answered many questions about illustrations and Higbee's.

I wish I could bestow a Royal Order of The Silver Grille Muffin on those who helped test the recipes in this book: The recipients would include: Jeanne Hudson, Jerry Maddox, Lori Ross, Carla Keller, Carolyn Dessin, Flo Worth Spencer, Michael D. Powell, Gerry Burdick, Cathy Brown, Janice Boggess, Marilyn Wilson, and Mary Sopinski. For this revision, Jane Hazen carefully reviewed all the recipes from the earlier edition just to make sure that they were correct. I also wish to thank Hunter Morrison, Cleveland's former director of city planning, for his contribution of the introduction to the original edition, which remains part of this one.

I also thank the people of Cleveland Landmarks Press, Dan and Kathy Cook, Greg and Liz Deegan, and especially Jim Toman for his help in editing the manuscript and preparing it for publication. Thanks as well to John Yasenosky for the map of Higbee's 10th floor, to William and Judi Moore for their ideas on cover design, and to Rusty Schneider of Moonlight Publishing for his work on the design and layout on both editions of the book.

Despite the assistance of these generous people, this project would not have moved forward without the constant encouragement and work of my wife, Judith, and the many contributions of Jane Hazen and of her husband Joseph Gagliotti, whose insights and culinary skill were of the highest importance.

For this revised edition, additional thanks are in order. I am grateful to James Richardson of Forest City Enterprises; John Williams, architect for the restoration; and Nancy McCann and Donald Beck, also of Forest City Enterprises, who have provided great assistance.

Richard E. Karberg
July 2002

Introduction

The sights, the sounds, the smells of Christmas. For many of us growing up in Cleveland in the 1950s, Higbee's department store offered all three. It was, indeed, a magical place. With the elaborate window displays, the lights, the grand high ceilinged main floor with its decorated chandeliers and long red carpet, the Twigbee Shop, and Santa Claus, Higbee's offered the rare mix of excitement and sophistication found only in the larger cities of New York and Chicago.

The Silver Grille was part of that experience. Like the rest of Higbee's at Christmas, it combined excitement and sophistication. A far cry from today's noisy mall food courts, The Silver Grille was a more mannered place, a place where, even for a child, lunch was an occasion, not just a pit stop.

This was as the Van Sweringen brothers had intended. Higbee's, and indeed the entire Terminal Tower group, was to be the urbane nexus of a new Cleveland–not the grimy mill town of the past, but the proud "Fifth City," the capital of a vast and booming Western Reserve region.

When The Higbee Company's new store opened in September 1931, it completed the ambitious Terminal Group, one of the first mixed-use developments in the country. Like the Cleveland Union Terminal at the center of the complex, Higbee's was a major anchor that drew people to downtown Cleveland. People came from throughout the region, by interurban, by trolley, by automobile, to spend the day shopping in the vast, well-appointed 12-story building.

And they were never disappointed. Higbee's management promoted its store as "the most convenient location in the city" and prided itself on perfecting the shopping experience. The artistry of visual display reached a high point at Higbee's, not only in the Christmas windows, but throughout the store–and throughout the year. Promotions and special events brought people together to attend lectures in its auditorium, meet the authors of popular books, and purchase exotic merchandise from Import Fairs. Christmas, of course, was the high point of the year, and The Silver Grille was an integral part of that experience.

When Higbee's opened its doors, it presented The Silver Grille, a tea room extraordinaire, whose extravagant art deco design extended from the space itself to the individual table settings. The menu, like the place, was elegant and appropriate, reflecting the tastes of the times.

The recipes in this book, assembled from the original recipe books preserved by former employees or left behind on the pantry shelves of The Silver Grille kitchen, bring back to life a forgotten cuisine. The recipes have been simplified and updated; favored ingredients of the time, such as lard, have been replaced, and the quantities have been reduced from "serves 50" to more reasonable numbers. But the tastes and spells of this bygone era have been retained.

Much as we Clevelanders have learned to take pride in our architectural heritage and have lovingly restored our grand spaces and historic buildings, we can also learn about and celebrate our shared cultural heritage as it is reflected in the food we once ate together.

Enjoy these recipes. And with them, remember the wonderful life of a seemingly simpler time.

Hunter Morrison

The response to the first edition of this book demonstrated that Greater Clevelanders had fond memories of The Higbee Company's Silver Grille restaurant. It went through seven printings, surprising even the authors with the power of the hold that the popular dining spot continued to have on its former patrons. After reading the book, many people eagerly shared their memories and memorabilia from this well-known dining spot. Yet everyone spoke of The Silver Grille as a phenomenon of the past, something that could only remain alive in memories, photographs, and other mementoes.

After the publication of *The Silver Grille: Memories and Recipes,* Allan Zambie of the John P. Murphy Foundation made available files, photographs, notebooks, and clippings collected by the late Herbert Strawbridge, who for many years led The Higbee Company. These valuable materials brought to light new information unavailable elsewhere. This cache of documents made possible the publication of a second book: *The Higbee Company and the Silver Grille: More Memories and Recipes.* This volume also received a warm welcome from the public.

The continuing demonstration of affection for The Silver Grille may have played some part in leading to the happy announcement by Forest City Enterprises, owner of Tower City Center and the Higbee Building, that it would restore and reopen The Silver Grille. For those many who thought The Silver Grille only belonged to our collective past, this announcement left us astounded. It was as if, contrary to the adage, one could really go home once again. Some doubted that it would really happen, especially after Dillard's decided to abandon its downtown store. But Forest City Enterprises was not deterred. Work went ahead as planned, and the "new" Silver Grille hosted its first event, a party for Leadership Cleveland, on May 11, 2002.

As work progressed on the restoration, it became apparent that this latest chapter in the history of the fabled dining spot should make its way into print. Thus this revised edition. What was contained in the original edition, anecdotes and recipes, is unchanged in this one. What has been added updates the original by describing the work that went into the restoration. That story is described in both word and picture. The photos illustrate various stages of the restoration and reveal how the "new edition" of the restaurant has remained faithful to the old.

As wonderful as memories can be, perhaps the only thing that can improve upon them is the real thing. The Silver Grille is back.

Richard E. Karberg
July 2002

This scene shows the Terminal Tower group, Higbee's at the left, the Tower in the center, and the Hotel Cleveland (now the Renaissance Cleveland Hotel) to the right–c.1950. *(Higbee Company photo, Jim Toman collection)*

The Silver Grille – My Story

I was born and raised in Cleveland at a time when shopping meant going downtown. It was a time before the advent of suburban shopping centers, when purchases of all sorts were made in the city's downtown department stores. And people didn't just come downtown to shop. They came to see doctors, conduct legal business, or perhaps to be entertained at the luxurious Palace, State, Ohio, Allen, or Stillman movie theaters at Playhouse Square, or at the Hippodrome on lower Euclid Avenue. In short, downtown was the place to go.

My mother was a smart shopper, always looking for bargains, and she knew when to shop for sales in Cleveland's department stores. And I was a fortunate son, for she frequently had me accompany her on her shopping forays, occasions I thoroughly enjoyed. Going downtown to shop was a production in those days. First, one had to be dressed properly, for shopping then was not the casual experience it has since become. Then there was the walk to the trolley stop, except for those rare occasions when my father was home during the day and he would chauffeur us to the portals of Higbee's.

It was a time when downtown Cleveland had many stores (in those days one used the word "stores" rather than "department stores"), but The Higbee Company was our favorite. We might also stop in at The May Company, and sometimes at Taylor's or Bailey's. Only at the end of the 1950s when family finances had improved and my mother had become more adventuresome, did we shop at the aristocratic Halle Bros. (not Brothers) Co. on the upper avenue.

Cleveland Railway Company and later CTS streetcars such as this one brought west siders downtown to shop at Higbee's and enjoy a meal in The Silver Grille. *(Bill Vigrass photo, Jim Toman collection)*

Serious shoppers had to make sure they were at the revolving doors of the store by 9:30 in order to be first in line for that day's bargains. In an era before outlet stores, every self-respecting homemaker felt it her duty to be a smart bargain shopper, and she would usually peruse the newspaper thoroughly before planning in detail her day's shopping strategy.

But for me, shopping was secondary. I felt that passing through the revolving doors into The Higbee Company's first floor was like coming into Fairyland. At the time of course, I knew nothing about art moderne, visual merchandising, or how store appointments were used to create the perfect environment for shopping, but I was enthralled nonetheless. The shiny marble floor, the high ceilings, and the banks of elevators (my mother would not use escalators) that whisked patrons up and down Higbee's 12 floors were for me the stuff of a dreamland.

Attached to Cleveland Union Terminal and the Terminal Tower, Higbee's had a great location, and inside, it had everything. Most people remember its large bargain basement with

Christmas time at The Higbee Company, Cleveland, Ohio

Higbee's always went all out to create stunning store decorations for the Christmas season. This postcard shows the street floor in 1946. *(Richard Karberg collection)*

The Higbee Company building had 74 display windows which were changed frequently. This Public Square window was decorated for the 1955 Christmas season, illustrating the attractive merchandise offered in the women's departments. *(Dillard's Department Stores)*

its wonderful frosty bar. Several additional floors were devoted to men's, women's, and children's clothing. Other floors featured a wonderful book shop, a stamp and coin department, home furnishings, toys, and even a large photo studio and an art gallery. On the 12th floor were pianos and musical instruments and a studio where children went for music lessons. Higbee's was a real adventure.

Higbee's had the cache of being upscale (before that word was understood)—it was almost like going to Halle's. Its window displays—there were 74 in all— served as an art museum experience for many Clevelanders, (especially at Christmas time). Higbee's was not only shopping; it was entertainment, art, and tradition. It always left me filled with wonder.

Of course, my mother and I did visit the other stores. They too had bargains to offer, but their much more pedestrian environment was certainly no match for what one experienced at Higbee's. It didn't take me long to cross these other stores off my list. They held no wonderland promise.

For me the high point of these downtown visits was lunch—lunch at the Higbee's restaurant. I soon became very familiar with that restaurant. A short ride in the elevator with an efficient—although sometimes snippy—young woman operator announcing the contents of each floor: "third floor better shoes, please step back, thank you"—brought us to the tenth floor and the art moderne (as today I recognize it) splendor of The Silver Grille. It was quiet and elegant, and the food was certainly to my liking. Lunching at The Silver Grille, not shopping, was my real motive for joining my mother on those downtown shopping excursions. Compared to The Silver Grille there was no other place to be.

The most elegant dining room in the Cleveland Union Terminal—and perhaps in the entire city—was the English Oak Room–circa 1935. Operated by Fred Harvey, the restaurant's excellent cuisine drew many Clevelanders for luncheon, dinner, late supper, or for special occasions. Now totally restored, the English Oak Room is used for special parties. *(Tower City Archives of Forest City Enterprises)*

A popular spot to find a quick lunch was the Fred Harvey fountain lunch counter on the Cleveland Union Terminal concourse–c. 1935. *(Tower City Archives of Forest City Enterprises)*

From time to time, of course, we would eat at other places downtown. Since I had a hearty appetite, I rated them satisfactory in the food category. Clark's on Euclid Avenue had great pies but a mediocre atmosphere. Sometimes to my distress we even ate at the lunch counter on the street floor of The May Company. I always felt cheated going there for lunch. I felt it had no class and was beneath what made for a true dining experience. Later I would visit May's Mayfair Room, which was not outstanding, and occasionally I would eat at the Minotaur Room at Halle Bros. The Minotaur Room had great murals, but little else of distinction.

Then in 1959 my family moved to Titusville, Florida, where we were seemingly on the frontier. There was no Higbee's, let alone a downtown. My time there was truly bleak, and I longed to get back to Cleveland, which held such rich memories for me.

By the time I returned to Cleveland in 1965, The Higbee Company had developed suburban branch stores. I thought they were pale reflections of the downtown store, and convenience aside, I always wondered why anyone would patronize them when the downtown store had so much more to offer. The suburban stores were not for me, and before I began my full-time teaching career, I landed a job as a contingent salesperson at Higbee's downtown. Once again I was in wonderland, and particularly so during the big fall and the Christmas shopping seasons. By then I had learned about architecture and the spirit of art deco, and I understood the role of the display people in contributing to the store's fanciful environment. As a Higbee employee I could enjoy that environment every day, and just upstairs, I could visit The Silver Grille as often as I wished, not just on occasional shopping trips. Those days have remained bright in my memory.

Shoppers wanting a quick lunch often patronized the lunch counter on the street floor of The May Company–1931. *(*Reprinted with permission from the *Plain Dealer*, © 1931; all rights reserved*)*

Later, having launched myself into my life's work (I began teaching in 1967) and having happily entered into marriage, I continued to patronize Higbee's and visit The Silver Grille. My wife Judith, who also appreciated the better things, enjoyed our lunches and dinners at The Silver Grille, and either through her own good judgment or my over-zealous influence, she too came to feel that the downtown Higbee store was the only place to shop—and the only place to have lunch.

When our children were old enough to take in the Higbee experience, we brought them along on our shopping trips, and we made sure, as occasions warranted, that they too had the opportunity to have lunch and dinner at The Silver Grille. By the 1980s I began to sense that these Higbee rituals would not last forever. It became all the more important to me that our children realize that going to The Silver Grille was a special event. I wanted very much for them to always be able to remember that magical place. When we traveled as a family, we would try the restaurants in other cities' department stores. My daughter Rebecca found her favorite in Chicago, the Walnut Room at Marshall Field's. The best for me, however, never changed. The Silver Grille remained tops.

Then on December 29, 1989, the unthinkable happened. The Silver Grille served its last meal. Times had changed, and the restaurant no longer represented a profit center for the department store, then being operated by the Dillard's chain. For many Clevelanders the restaurant retained a strong sentimental attraction, but nostalgia was not enough to keep its doors open. A wonderful Cleveland tradition became a memory.

Those memories kept drawing me back. As a photographer I tried to record what once had been so central to the downtown shopping era. Then in more recent years, as I engaged in research on Cleveland architecture, I again had the opportunity of visiting the unique space that was once The Silver Grille. Out of those visits the intent to write this book slowly formed.

The Higbee Company Store

In 1931 two outstanding structures at opposite ends of Euclid Avenue opened. Both were designed in a version of the stripped classical style, and both exhibited unparalleled use of color and other aspects of design. Both featured the latest in mechanical and technical systems. The first of these structures was Severance Hall located at University Circle. Designed by the Cleveland firm of Walker and Weeks, Severance Hall was built as the home of the Cleveland Orchestra, and today it basks in recognition as an ultimate achievement in a building designed for high culture.

Severance Hall retained its neoclassic lines following the addition and restoration work which was completed in January 2000. *(Jim Toman photo)*

The second building to open was The Higbee Company department store at Public Square. The building was designed by the Chicago firm of Graham, Anderson, Probst and White, architects for the Terminal Tower project. The Higbee Company store completed the Public Square frontage of the Terminal project which had been initiated in 1918 by Oris Paxton and Mantis James Van Sweringen as a daring commercial redevelopment of downtown. The Terminal project was also the city's transportation center for both the mainline railroad passenger service and for the rapid transit lines which linked downtown to the Van Sweringen suburban developments in Shaker Heights and adjacent areas.

The Higbee Building harmonizes well with the rest of the Terminal complex in overall design, height, and other external aspects, but as one of the last phases of construction, its design incorporated a good deal of the modernism which in the 1920s was coming into vogue in American architecture.

The Higbee building is under construction in 1930. The view is of the Prospect and Ontario corner. *(Higbee Company photo, Jim Toman collection)*

It may seem inappropriate to compare a commercial building with the renowned Severance Hall, but each in its own way reflected the latest in design while still being true to its purpose. Both buildings reflected a sense of luxury in their design and execution. They were statements in stone and steel that Cleveland was a wealthy and powerful city, confident of its destiny not only as a regional center but one able to command national and even international attention. Both were planned in the late 1920s when it was felt that economic prosperity would go on forever. Both represented the hopes and dreams of leading Cleveland families, who like their counterparts in New York and London, were lords of their dreams.

The two buildings, however, were not equally favored by history. Severance Hall still continues its rich cultural tradition, and its prominence was made even more lustrous by the stellar addition and renovation which took place in 1998-1999. The Higbee Company building, on the other hand, fell on hard times as the changing face of commerce made its original purpose somewhat obsolete.

The Higbee Company began in 1858 as Hower and Higbee, with a store just off Public Square. In 1910 the firm moved to a new building at the northwest corner of Euclid Avenue and East 13th Street, the area which then was considered the choice for the carriage trade. There it became an able competitor to the larger and more elegant Halle Bros. Co. store just across the avenue.

Before its move to Public Square, The Higbee Company was located in this four story building on Euclid Avenue at East 13th Street. It later became home for the consolidated Sterling Lindner Davis Company. *(Higbee Company photo, Jim Toman collection)*

The size of the Higbee store (building at right-with air conditioning units on the roof) is apparent in this aerial view, when compared to the slender profile of the Terminal Tower Building, to its left - 1950. *(Robert Runyon photo, Bruce Young collection)*

An early postcard scene provides a night-time view of the Terminal Tower group. The Higbee store, at the lower left, was its own beacon for shoppers. *(Richard Karberg collection)*

My grandmother remembered The Higbee Company at that location, and the store's penchant for hiring clerks who were more haughty than those at Halle's—a firm indicator of the store's elevated social reputation. Higbee's on Euclid Avenue was a class act.

In the boom period of the 1920s Higbee's was bursting at the seams. It added two more floors to display and sell luxury goods. The store attempted to promote elegance, fashion, and artistic taste. Asa Shiverick headed the store in the 1920s along with William T. Higbee, son of the store's founder and an accomplished photographer. When photographer Margaret Bourke White arrived in Cleveland from Cornell, Shiverick hired her to photograph the store's display windows.

In the 1920s the Van Sweringen brothers were searching for a tenant to anchor the final piece of their Public Square development. As told by Asa Shiverick, Jr., the Vans went door to door on Euclid Avenue asking store owners to consider moving into the Terminal Tower development. They found a receptive listener in Shiverick, who agreed to move the store closer to its historic roots. On September 8, 1931, The Higbee Company moved into its new Public Square headquarters. The 12-floor, one-million-square-foot store gave the company room to grow. It was the largest department store to open in the U.S. in the previous 20 years, and almost everything inside it was new, including the $5 million in merchandise that was ready for shoppers eager to experience the new Higbee's.

The features of the Higbee building have been recounted elsewhere, but little has been written about its restaurants. Tea rooms and restaurants were essential parts of department stores during this era. Shopping was hard and serious business, and this meant that women, as well as the occasional male shopper, would spend almost an entire day at the task before rushing home to be sure the evening meal would be served on time. These shoppers needed sustenance to carry on with the task.

In this era the only respectable eating places for women were hotel dining rooms. The problem was that these hotels were not always close to stores, and meals were therefore time consuming as well as expensive. Department stores realized they could fill a need for food, make their customers happy, and provide a break so they would return to the sales floors refreshed and primed to purchase even more merchandise.

THE HIGBEE CO.

Trifle and Treasure

For the Bride's House

...from the Higbee Fifth Floor China and Glass Section

"LOWESTOFT"

29-piece tea service for eight by Spode..150.00

In the rare gray of early Chinese porcelain! Oriental floral center medallions flanked by geometric English border, richly gold embellished. In that precious class of "keep forever's"!

Service includes: *teapot with braided handle, covered sugar jar with braided handles, Chinese Chippendale pitcher, eight plates, eight gracious cups, eight "deep-dish" saucers*

LENOX "PRISCILLA" CHINA

Pale transulscent ivory banded in a fragile Lenox-blue forget-me-not, bordered with fine fan-fluting! Complete services in this charming pattern are available.

cups and saucers **40.00** dozen
dinner plates **40.00** dozen
service plates deeply banded in "Lenox-blue" **60.00** dozen

★

Note: Our collection of Irish Belleck is most comprehensive, in service and decorative pieces.

"Diamond Band" Stemware by Hunt

A complete series of stemware with a distinctly Federal flavour achieved by double rows of hand-cut "diamond" banding! **25.00**

Hunt Crystal Bowl and Candelabras

Brilliantly clear crystal deeply hand-faceted in a radiant sunburst and thumb-print design! Low broad bowl and two, two-branch candlebra each shining with twenty hand-cut prisms! **38.00**

When the Higbee Company was located on East 13th Street and Euclid Avenue, its merchandise was limited to men's and women's apparel. Its spacious Public Square location allowed it to become a full department store, as these early advertisements (above and facing) attest. *(The Higbee Company, Richard Karberg collection)*

THE HIGBEE CO.

We've Made Your Bed...You Lie on it
Luxuriously!

We really believe we have one of the loveliest collections of blankets, comforts and bedspreads in America...the sort that ordinarily you would find only in the most exclusive Fifth Avenue shops in New York! They're out-of-the-ordinary . . . made of the most exquisite materials . . . designed to add to an atmosphere of gracious living.

The taffeta spread shown has every tiny stitch taken by hand—note the beautiful quilted design of the top. **16.95**

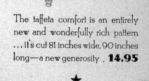

The taffeta comfort is an entirely new and wonderfully rich pattern ...it's cut 81 inches wide, 90 inches long—a new generosity . **14.95**

★

St. Marys makes the loveliest blankets in the world, we think— as is witnessed by this fluffy one in three tones **14.95**

• FOURTH FLOOR •

The Silver Grille

Stepping out of the elevator on the 10th floor, Higbee customers entered the richly paneled lobby designed by Philip Small which served as the perfect prelude to the elegance of The Silver Grille—1989. *(Richard Karberg photo)*

The original design of the new Higbee store was to include two restaurant spaces on the 11th floor of the building. One area was to be a tea room. Adjacent to it, plans called for an octangular men's smoking room. A corridor would lead to a large formal restaurant twice the size of the tea room. Two banks of elevators would bring patrons to these restaurants and the auditorium. The facilities could also be reached by a passageway which connected directly with the Terminal Tower. These were the plans in April 1930. A few months later, however, designers unveiled a new set of plans with an auditorium, restaurant, and tea room on the tenth floor. This floor had no direct connection with the Terminal Tower, so it was to be reached by the elevators or by two banks of escalators from the street floor. The plans for August 1930 indicate the still-unnamed tea room as designed in a neo-classic Adamesque style with columns topped with Ionic capitals and austere wall finishes. The adjacent restaurant was accessed via sets of French doors and was to be paneled and crowned by a glass ceiling.

Plans changed again, and the tea room, later to be named The Silver Grille, was designed in the art moderne style, sometimes also called "steamship modern," since it was often employed in the design of such ocean liners of the late 1920s and early 1930s as the *Empress of Britain*, the *Queen Mary*, and the *Normandie*.

Philip Small of the Cleveland firm of Small and Rowley designed The Silver Grille space. This was one of the Van Sweringens' favorite architectural firms. Because of its chummy relationship with the Vans, this firm was also chosen to design the Terminal Tower's interior spaces, complete the Moreland Courts apartments on Shaker Boulevard, as well as to redesign the Vans' house on South Park Boulevard and their country house, Daisy Hill, in Hunting Valley. They also designed Shaker Square.

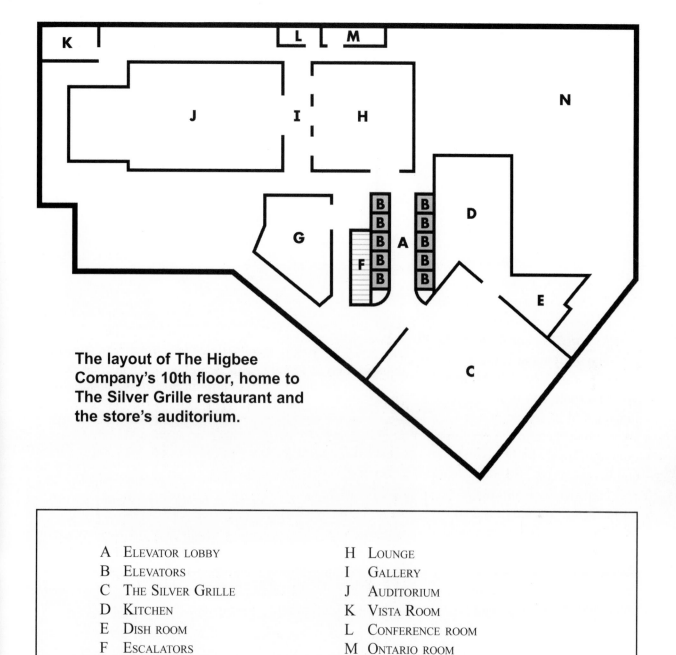

The layout of The Higbee Company's 10th floor, home to The Silver Grille restaurant and the store's auditorium.

A	Elevator lobby	H	Lounge
B	Elevators	I	Gallery
C	The Silver Grille	J	Auditorium
D	Kitchen	K	Vista Room
E	Dish room	L	Conference room
F	Escalators	M	Ontario room
G	Pronto room	N	Higbee display studio

The furniture was by William Green and Andrew Probala of Rorimer-Brooks, who designed furniture for some of Cleveland's most discriminating families as well as for the Statler Hotel chain, the Greenbrier, the Cleveland Playhouse, and the Vans' home at Daisy Hill. The tables and chairs were made of aluminum by General Fireproofing of Youngstown, Ohio. The table tops, originally black in color, were an early use of Formica.

The china, designed to complement the architecture of the room, was supervised by Guy Cowan, who had once operated the famed Cowan Pottery in Rocky River and then worked for Syracuse China in Syracuse, New York. Table linens also echoed the art deco design of the room.

When the store opened, the *Plain Dealer* reviewed the design features of the building. In speaking of The Silver Grille the paper said:

> In the tea room Small has used six shades of green in the decoration combined with a silver leaf pattern. Door, window fixtures and furnishings including tables and chairs are in aluminum. For the fountain in the center of the room Small selected slabs of Rojo alicante marble, color features of which is near perfect.

The unifying effect is a triumph of understated elegance.

The room was designed so lunch could be served in a refined atmosphere to the accompaniment of music by Louis Rich and his orchestra. Because swing was considered uncultured, guests heard soft renditions of popular songs, what later would be termed "schmaltz." Fashion shows, which presented the latest Parisian styles, helped entice exhausted shoppers to visit the women's salons on the third floor.

Lillian Beck, who began as a waitress in The Silver Grille in 1935, recalls that the service was in keeping with the best restaurants of the time. This was an era flavored by the use of finger bowls, after-dessert mints served on Silver Grille china, and a cheese board at meal's end. Christmas dinners served during this period usually featured an entrée of prime rib with Yorkshire pudding.

The Silver Grille was decorated to coordinate with special events, such as Import Fairs, one of which is seen in this view from the late 1970s. *(Margaret Halterlein collection)*

The Silver Grille's tables and chairs were designed by the firm of Rorimer-Brooks. *(Ramon Pina photo, 1989, courtesy of Leslie Pina)*

A dinner plate in the Higbee Company pattern designed by Syracuse China in 1931. This pattern was used until the 1960s. *(The Higbee Company)*

The Silver Grille is seen at the time The Higbee Company opened its new Public Square store—September 8, 1931. *(Cleveland* Press *Collection of the Cleveland State University archives)*

Both Beck and another veteran waitress, Lottie Jenc, recall that during the 1930s Silver Grille patrons were on equal social footing with those who frequented the Halle Bros. Co. The Silver Grille became a lunch destination for society women (such as Mrs. Harvey Firestone, who some waitresses considered a poor tipper) and luminaries who came to the store for book talks and other special events. Other guests included O.P. and M. J. Van Sweringen, who were remembered as kind and courteous but reserved. The Higbee executives of the era, including William T. Higbee, Charles Bradley, and John Murphy, would frequently eat in The Silver Grille and were admired because they always appeared to know the waitresses.

Lunch guests could also come from their offices in the Terminal Tower. A 13th floor passageway in the Tower connected to what was Higbee's 12th floor, which was at this time the entrance to WHK Radio, which occupied the uppermost floors of the Higbee Building.

During the 1930s, when the wage was 25¢ an hour and a good tip was a quarter for four people, the most often requested entrees were creamed chicken, chicken pie, or Welsh rarebit.

The Higbee waitresses were also kept busy helping in the private dining rooms in the Guildhall Building across Prospect Avenue, which were managed by the formidable Mrs. Kenneth McKay, who also ran The Silver Grille.

The main restaurant planned adjacent to The Silver Grille was never built. As the depression worsened, there were cutbacks in the plans for the Higbee Building. Additional escalators and other features were not built. It was hoped that as economic conditions improved, these amenities could be included, but they never did appear. In the meantime The Silver Grille served lunch and dinner as well as tea from its large kitchen which had been originally designed to serve two eating spaces. Eventually the space reserved for the main restaurant was given over to the large and important display department.

The Silver Grille was an instant success. On opening day, September 8, 1931, it was packed, and over the next 58 years it continued to draw large crowds.

In 1962 Raymond Loewy and William Snaith updated The Silver Grille's design by adding a lighter color scheme and adding banquettes which increased the room's capacity to 550. When asked about the cost of the renovation, John P. Murphy, who headed the store at the time, replied that cost was not the important issue. What was important was that The Silver Grille remained one of the most attractive rooms in the country.

Higbee's had other eating places, but none could match The Silver Grille. During special events such as meetings, fashion shows, and private parties, meals were served in four smaller rooms, the auditorium, and the lounge. Smaller eating areas were also established in the form of an ice cream parlor on the 8th floor and a Bistro on the 2nd floor. Many shoppers entering the store from the Cleveland Union Terminal concourse or looking for bargains in the basement store stopped at the Frosty Bar, which served a frosted malted milk drink which had an almost cult-like following. In 1960 the store introduced the Pronto Room on the 10th

Higbee's Pronto Room during some of the store's Import Fairs received extra decorations to mark the occasion–c.1960. *(Higbee Company photo)*

The Frosty Bar at the entrance to Higbee's Basement Store from the Terminal Tower concourse was a welcoming stop for a Frosty Freeze or a quick snack–1975. *(Ann Zupancic photo)*

floor. During the famous Import Fairs special menus were devised for both the lounge and the Pronto Room. During much of the rest of the year the Pronto Room served a limited selection of set meals on trays reminiscent of airline fare.

The famous Higbee Company sign above the Public Square marquee survived until 1989, when Dillard's took over the store's operation and discontinued the use of all the floors above the fourth level. *(Jack Muslovski photo, Jim Toman collection)*

The Silver Grille Experience

The Silver Grille was more than food. It played an important role in the merchandising ideas of The Higbee Company. At special times of the year, but especially before Christmas, The Silver Grille would be jammed with children who had been brought downtown for breakfast with Santa or perhaps for a holiday lunch before or after seeing Santa, Bruce the Spruce, or in later years, Mr. Jingeling. As many as 5,000 would be served in the Higbee restaurants on the day after Thanksgiving or on a Saturday during the Christmas shopping season. The famous Toyland, which in the 1930s occupied the entire 7th floor, was another attraction. A flavor of this experience is captured in the film, *A Christmas Story,* in which Ralphie gets to tell Santa his wish for a Red Ryder Air Rifle after seeing one amid the Toyland fantasy in the Higbee corner window.

When ready for a break from shopping, the family would board an operator-controlled elevator (all elevator operators wore identical uniforms which changed with the season). The elevator starter, who controlled all 20 lifts, would point

When it opened, Higbee's had 20 passenger elevators which took patrons from the basement store up to the 11th floor. All required elevator operators, who were hired for their good looks as well as for their ability to operate the lifts. (*Cleveland* Press *Collection of the Cleveland State University Archives*)

Silver Grille-goers to the express car which would whisk them non-stop to the 10th floor lobby. Reservations were not usually taken, so patrons would have to wait in line according to the size of their group. Once their turn came, the door lady would direct them to one of the hostesses, who in turn would usher them to a table and hand them menus, with special menus for the children. Coats and shopping bags were not a problem because Higbee's provided a hospitality suite and checked parcels and wraps free of charge. Higbee management realized that at this point the patrons were not merely store customers. They had been raised to the higher station of being a guest for lunch, tea, or dinner.

Once seated, a guest could not help but recognize the integration of table design, table settings, and the elegant features of the room itself. The color scheme changed from silver and green to brighter and more metallic tones, but even if people did not know the fancy terms for the colors and appointments, they surely appreciated the elegance and unity of the aesthetics. Food and service were faithful to a high standard. Such was The Silver Grille experience.

A family is seated in The Silver Grille during Christmas season 1980. The cardboard stove was always a treat for the children–and sometimes for the parents too. *(Ann Zupancic photo)*

Children in a high pitch of excitement would bolt from their seats and run to the pond surrounding the fountain and watch the famous goldfish. After they returned to their tables, The Silver Grille tradition was to serve the children's meals in what early on were called buffets containing tiny ceramic dishes along with silverware and a napkin. During the Christmas period these meals were brought in miniature stoves. These stoves and buffets are now prized icons of a vanished childhood, and adults of a certain age fondly remember them. By 1974 the wooden buffets and metal

Children's Book Department, Prospect Level - c.1940. (*Cleveland* Press *Collection of the Cleveland State University Archives*)

stoves, for reasons of economy and hygiene, were replaced by cardboard toy stoves which were given out to all children. In 1983 Jim McConnell, director of food services for Higbee's, introduced a toy cardboard truck which he felt would be more appealing to boys.

It was hoped that a Silver Grille visit would revive patrons so that they could continue shopping. Some patrons, however, though their appetite had been appeased, would still be too exhausted for more shopping. If they were homeward bound, they could board the elevator for a trip to the bargain basement, where they could conveniently exit to the Cleveland Union Terminal to catch a rapid transit, or to follow the passage to the indoor Huron Road garage to retrieve their car. Shopping at Higbee's had much to commend it.

By the 1950s Higbee executives realized that in an era of rapid suburbanization, incentives and promotions would be necessary to continue to bring shoppers to the downtown store.

Higbee's officials accordingly developed a number of ideas to lure people to their downtown store. Starting in fall 1953, a series of Import Fairs attracted people to see previously unavailable merchandise. An Ohiorama in the summer brought people to the store during what was traditionally a slow shopping season. Events scheduled for the 10th floor auditorium also brought people to the restaurants. Serving all of these hungry people at lunch, tea, or dinner was an important part of the Higbee tradition.

Many events spilled over into The Silver Grille. It would be festively decorated at Christmas and for the special promotions. Informal modeling was one of the features that made Silver Grille dining even more interesting for patrons. So both through promotion and in decor, The Silver Grille became an integral part of The Higbee Company's sales approach.

The Higbee display staff created spectacular settings for the store's special promotions, such as this setting on the street floor celebrating a Texas connection–c.1980. *(Higbee Company photo, Jim McConnell collection)*

The Silver Grille Employees

While The Silver Grille provided meals day in and day out at Higbee's for over 58 years, its peak operations occurred during the 1930s and 1940s when its kitchen employed 60 to 70 people. In an era prior to the advent of ready-to-eat foods, it was necessary to prepare all the fruits and vegetables, bake all of the breads, rolls, and cakes and to make sauces and stocks and soups within the kitchen. The kitchen staff was all female, with the majority of the women from the West Side Irish community, and those in the dish room of Italian descent.

The day began early for the kitchen staff. They would arrive by 7:00 a.m., turn on the steam lines, light the gas ovens, and start to work. Their day ended about 4:30 p.m.

Carolyn Taylor, who was in charge of Higbee restaurants from 1975 to 1983, recalled that it was an awesome daily task to prepare meals from scratch for a 500-seat restaurant. She remembered the kitchen employees as "hard working and very happy people." When the Pronto Room was also in operation, and especially during the import fairs in the lounge or during auditorium events, the spacious kitchen was used to capacity.

In 1974 the day begins for The Silver Grille waitresses with a meeting. The waitresses are wearing their newly created yellow uniforms. *(The Higbee Company, Richard Karberg collection)*

At its peak the staff required in The Silver Grille included 75 waitresses. In the 1930s busboys were also a part of the staff. The March 1957 *Higbee News and Views*, the employee magazine, published a photograph of mother-daughter waitresses in The Silver Grille. Ann Zupancic recalls that being a waitress was often a family affair. Many of them saw their daughters—sometimes as many as three daughters—or sisters-in-law work alongside while sons would sometimes come in after school to work in the dish room. The Silver Grille had that kind of appeal. By the 1980s the number of waitresses was reduced to half of what it had been in the restaurant's heyday.

Waitresses were expected to be at work by 10:00 a.m. to set the tables and arrange the room for the lunch crowd. Originally each waitress was assigned only two or three tables; later that number was increased. Some of the waitresses were part time, while others worked the set-up in the morning, and then stayed through lunch, tea, and dinner on evenings when the store remained open late. There were occasions when some of the

In 1980 a Silver Grille kitchen employee is busy preparing desserts, a menu feature for which the restaurant was justly famous. *(Ann Zupancic photo)*

One of the veteran Silver Grille kitchen employees is enjoying her work —1974. *(Ann Zupancic photo)*

waitresses would leave immediately after lunch to attend a movie or stage show at the Palace or State theaters at Playhouse Square, or to shop at one of the other downtown department stores. Angela Mylen, a veteran Silver Grille waitress, recalls leaving early on fall Saturdays to watch her future husband, then a student at Adelbert College, play on the Western Reserve University football team.

Being a waitress at The Silver Grille was considered a desirable position. Mrs. Kenneth McKay (Kenneth was her given first name, and she was English) hired the waitresses, and she was considered a stern and demanding employer. A beginning waitress had classes every morning for two weeks and then shadowed another waitress before she was allowed onto the floor by herself. Veteran waitress Lottie Jenc remembered the training as rigorous and intimidating. She said the waitresses, however, ultimately realized it was a good experience and came to appreciate it. Recruits came from a pool who already had some experience. Many came from other downtown restaurants. Higbee's was easily accessible by public transportation from most parts of the county, and the store discount was an added attraction. The job seemed to breed loyalty. Many waitresses remained on the job for 40 years, some having arrived on opening day in 1931.

The waitress staff was augmented by what were called party ladies. Party ladies were women from a society background who worked at special events in the Auditorium, banquet rooms, or lounge. The proceeds they earned were applied to the organizations they represented, such as garden clubs and other charities.

Informal modeling took place during luncheon in The Silver Grille. Here a Silver Grille patron admires the latest fashions for fall–1958. *(Cleveland* Press *Collection of the Cleveland State University Archives)*

Margaret Halterlein (left), the last Silver Grille manager, Jim McConnell, (second from left), Higbee's last food service manager, and other Silver Grille employees catered an event on the presidential yacht *Sequoia*, after it docked in Cleveland in 1985. *(Jim McConnell collection)*

It was a good way for organizations to raise money. They also enjoyed working at Higbee's because it allowed them to participate at close range in noteworthy events and meet famous individuals who were scheduled to appear in the Auditorium. One such event was a talk by Amelia Earhart, opening the Auditorium in 1932.

And there were many more like it. Among the most popular were events presented jointly with the Higbee book department, which were regular features from the 1950s through the 1970s. Richard Gildenmeister, who was then part of the book department, recalls some of these events. One book-related Auditorium event launched *I Laughed, I Cried, I Loved*, a book by popular local television personality, Dorothy Fuldheim. The program was televised live by Cleveland station WEWS and attended by a crowd of 900 who lunched on Silver Grille-prepared cuisine.

Theodore Seuss Geisel (known to children as Dr. Seuss) was featured in another Auditorium event. The Silver Grille staff prepared a breakfast for the attending children. The menu featured food items made famous in the Seuss series of books.

Other famous authors who lunched at The Silver Grille included Lillian Gish, who "adored" its food, Anita Loos, David Frost, and Irving Stone. To be a part of these events had a certain cache about it.

Supervising the hustle and bustle of seating guests were five ladies. One, stationed at the front of The Silver Grille, supervised the long line of those waiting to be seated—sometimes out of necessity with the precision of a military commander. She, in turn, would direct the next in line to one of her four sub-lieutenants stationed around the room. It was an efficient and yet refined system.

Tea was served in the afternoon in The Silver Grille until the early 1980s. But by then women had rejoined the workforce in large numbers, and the nature of coming downtown to shop had changed. Shopping became a less leisurely but more practical experience. Tea then required only a small number of waitresses.

The Silver Grille kitchen staff was mostly composed of loyal, long-term employees. Ann Zupancic is fourth from the left—1947. *(Ann Zupancic collection)*

Defining the Tea Room

The Silver Grille was classified as a tea room in the multi-level dining universe. By definition, tea room food was considered more dainty, was served in smaller portions, and it was fussy. Some might have viewed it as "ladies' fare," while others might have considered it prototypical WASP cooking. In the early part of the 20th century, convention had it that middle class women ate less, ate more slowly, and ate foods that were refined. The color, texture, and presentation of food items were considered as important as the ingredients themselves. Alcoholic beverages were frowned upon, and were not to be found on a tea room menu. The fact that the Silver Grille opened during Prohibition made that an irrelevant issue. It was not until the early 1980s that a bar was finally established there.

Probably the highest offering in the shrine of tea room cuisine was chicken a la king. When prepared properly and served on good biscuits, it still remains a favorite on the list of what is now termed "comfort food." Because it has so often been ill-prepared, served in cardboard pastry shells or with soggy rice or noodles, this entree has earned as many disparaging comments as another tea room favorite, chipped beef on toast. Other foods such as gelatin salads, Welsh rarebit, creamed eggs and tomatoes, and a huge listing of delicious desserts form part of the tea room culinary catalog. Many of the original Silver Grille recipes remained on the menu throughout the restaurant's prime.

The Silver Grille fountain was decorated appropriately for the seasons of the year. This arrangement represented early spring—1983. *(Richard Karberg photo)*

Absent from the menu were foods which reflected ethnic or regional differences. During its first 50 years, there was not a single hamburger, pizza, taco, stir fry, or a multitude of other items now considered standard, on the menus of The Silver Grille. Such items made their first appearance on Silver Grille menus in the 1980s in order to accommodate the changes in taste and economics of those who ate out. At the same time, theme luncheons and buffets and salad bars had their debut in The Silver Grille.

But in the earlier tea room mode, meats were served in sauces or gravy, accompanied by salads and stewed vegetables and the famous Higbee muffins. Tempting desserts were popular attractions during an era blissfully ignorant of cholesterol concerns.

The person who created the original menus and recipes was Mrs. Kenneth McKay. Other recipes came from the famous Schrafft's Restaurant chain in New York, probably the best known chain of tea rooms in the nation. A 1933 article in *Business Week* about Schrafft's stated that the Schrafft's formula was high quality rigidly controlled. Chicken was the favorite dish at Schrafft's at the time. *Business Week* also commented that women played a large part in the development of the Schrafft's organization. McKay ably transplanted these aspects of the business to Higbee's in Cleveland. Chicken was so central to the menu that one kitchen staff member's job was to do nothing other than remove the meat from the bones.

The only departure from a strict tea room menu came on the occasions when The Silver Grille remained opened for dinner. Then a different menu, with larger portions and steak and prime rib roast, appeared.

The tea room era was a time when if one wanted Italian or Chinese food, he or she went to an Italian or Chinese restaurant (although such venues were then not considered respectable for ladies dining unattended). Mexican food, so popular today, was then considered much too exotic.

Tea rooms existed in most American department stores. Many department stores, and of course their tea rooms as divisions of these enterprises, banded together into the American Merchandising Corporation (AMC) which shared recipes and operational ideas for their tea rooms. The famed Maurice salad and dressing was a product of this affiliation, and in addition to Higbee's it was available at J .L. Hudson, Lazarus, Marshall Fields, and other well-known stores.

In those days department stores prided themselves on their tea rooms. Today only a few still exist. One of the legendary restaurants of this period still in existence is the Walnut Room at the Marshall Fields store on State Street in Chicago, which is now probably in many ways the Queen Mother of all department store restaurants. In New York, Lord and Taylor and B. Altman were known for their tea rooms. Across urban America there were many popular icons to the kind of food and refined atmosphere which only a proper tea room could provide. In Cleveland, The Silver Grille did it best.

Afternoon Tea
50¢

Banana Bread with Cream Cheese
Nut Ball and Tea

❀

Toasted Orange Bread
with Cream Cheese and Tea

❀

Buttered Cinnamon Toast Sticks
and Tea

Sandwiches

Higbee-Special Sandwich
(Swiss Cheese, Canadian Bacon,
White Meat of Turkey, Russian
Dressing and Garnish of Tomato
and Sliced Egg) 1.00
Sliced White Meat of Chicken . . . 1.10
Baked Ham Sandwich on Rye Bread,
with Pickle Sticks 75
Chicken or Tunafish Salad Sandwich
on White or Rye Bread 75
Bacon, Lettuce and Tomato on Toast . .90

Hot Entrees

Welsh Rarebit on Melba
Toast with Almonds and
a Salad of Fresh Fruit
Sections with Roll . . . 1.00
Scrambled Eggs and
Cheese with Shoestring
Potatoes and Sliced
Tomatoes with Roll . . .85
Chicken Pie with Pastry
Crust and a Fresh Fruit
Salad with Roll . . . 1.20
Fried Ham Steak, French
Fried Potatoes, Sliced
Tomatoes and a Roll 1.25
Chopped Beef Steak
on a Toasted Bun with
Relish, Catsup and
French Fried Potatoes . .90

Special Salads

Special Fruit Salad made
with Sections of the
Season's Freshest Fruits,
Complemented by our
own Glacé Dressing . . 1.00
Higbee Mixed Salad:
Lettuce, Tomato,
Avocado Pear, Celery,
Sliced Egg, Anchovy
and-Roquefort Cheese
Dressing 1.00
Salad of Fresh Greens
Tossed with Julienne
Ham, Swiss Cheese
and French or
Russian Dressing . . . 1.00
Yellow Cling Peach
Halves with Creamed
Cottage Cheese, Crisp
Shredded Lettuce,
Glacé Dressing 85

☆   ☆   ☆

Served with Roll and Butter
or
Melba Toast

Sweets

Fresh Homebaked
Apple Pie 30
Cake of the Day 30
Pie of the Day 30

Fountain Features

Toasted Pecan Ball
with Fudge Sauce . . .40
Coconut Ice Cream Ball
with Butterscotch Sauce .35
Toasted Almond Ice Cream
Ball with Butterscotch
Sauce 35
Maple Pecan Parfait . . .40
Chocolate Nut Parfait . . .40
Chocolate Milk Shake . . .35
Chocolate Malted Milk . .40
Chocolate Soda 30
Pineapple, Butterscotch,
Cold Fudge or Chocolate
Marshmallow Sundae . .30
Boston Cooler with
Root Beer 30
Root Beer, Gingerale,
Pepsi-Cola or Lemonade .20
Vanilla, Chocolate, Mint,
Coffee or Peppermint
Ice Cream 20
Pineapple, Orange or
Raspberry Sherbet . . .20

Beverages

Iced Coffee or Tea 20
Pot of Coffee 20
Pot of Tea 20
Pot of Hot Chocolate
with Whipped Cream . .25

**The Afternoon Tea menu offered many tempting items to sustain a Higbee shopper until dinner
time.** *(Margaret Halterlein collection)*

SCHRAFFT'S

THE
LOUNGE
MENU

Other Stores and Tea Rooms
Broadway & 37th Street
Fifth Avenue, & 38th Street
56 Liberty Street
35 Nassau Street
416 Fulton St., Brooklyn

Fifty-Four
West Twenty-Third Street
New York City

A menu from Schrafft's Restaurant in New York City, the chain that popularized the tea room experience. *(Richard Karberg collection)*

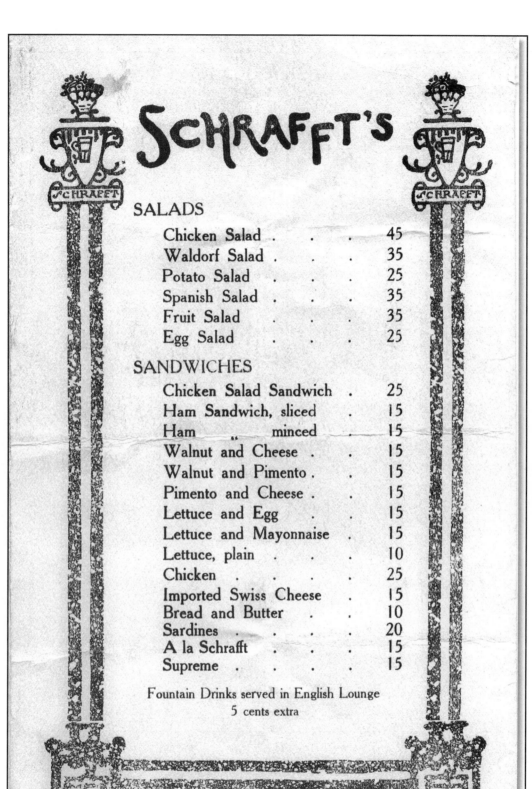

SCHRAFFT'S

SALADS

Chicken Salad . . .	45
Waldorf Salad . . .	35
Potato Salad . . .	25
Spanish Salad . . .	35
Fruit Salad . . .	35
Egg Salad . . .	25

SANDWICHES

Chicken Salad Sandwich .	25
Ham Sandwich, sliced .	15
Ham " minced .	15
Walnut and Cheese . .	15
Walnut and Pimento . .	15
Pimento and Cheese . .	15
Lettuce and Egg . .	15
Lettuce and Mayonnaise .	15
Lettuce, plain . . .	10
Chicken . . .	25
Imported Swiss Cheese .	15
Bread and Butter . .	10
Sardines . . .	20
A la Schrafft . . .	15
Supreme . . .	15

Fountain Drinks served in English Lounge
5 cents extra

What Happened to The Silver Grille

By the late 1970s Higbee management had become quite aware of the major changes taking place in shopping patterns as well as in the public's use of downtown Cleveland. Certainly office buildings remained quite well occupied by leading firms. The courts, banks, accounting firms, and other corporate offices continued to draw many people to downtown Cleveland during business hours. Other activities downtown, however, began to languish. One by one the theaters on Euclid Avenue closed. Some were demolished, and others more happily were saved to form the dynamic new Playhouse Square development.

Shopping downtown also changed. Long-time retailers such as Bonwit Teller and Sterling Lindner, with its famous court and equally famous Christmas tree, were no longer in business. Their departure continued a trend started in 1961 with the closure of the William Taylor and Sons department store, followed just months later by The Bailey Company. Increased competition from suburban branches of the traditional downtown stores and from new retailers elsewhere brought about the end of the dominance of downtown as a shopping center.

The loss of retail business and the closure of the theaters began a downward spiral, aggravated by a perceived rise of crime in the downtown area. Downtown Cleveland was in serious trouble.

Higbee's remained in business because of the breadth of its merchandise, its effective promotions, and its strategic Public Square location. And The Silver Grille continued to play an integral part in store officials' plans. In 1974, the restaurant received a makeover, giving it a more contemporary feel. An emerald green, white, and daffodil yellow color motif was reflected in the appointments and in seven new wall murals.

By 1980 Higbee store executives realized that the million square feet of space in its elegant building had become far more than was necessary for running a complete downtown store in a city which was experiencing an economic downturn and a continuing loss of population. Even the closure of the Halle Bros. store in 1982 did not generate new business for Higbee's, and store management wisely shunned offers to open a branch in the Halle Building. Instead it began plans to consolidate sales areas and offer part of the square footage on its upper floors for office use by Standard Oil Company of Ohio (Sohio) and Women's Federal Savings and Loan, which had outgrown their own office space in nearby buildings. In 1983 Higbee executives even considered transforming The Silver Grille into a salad bar, and a smaller crystal room, but instead the restaurant was treated to its third redecoration, one which better suited its original art deco styling. Muted colors in the wallpaper, carpeting, and upholstery gave the room a more traditional ambiance.

The purchase of a large block of Higbee stock by Industrial Equities of New Zealand in 1983 brought increased pressure on Higbee management to run a tighter ship, especially at its downtown location. Over the years, The Silver Grille typically operated at a loss, with the possible exception of the Christmas season. Because the restaurant was part of the Higbee tradition of service and promotion, the thought of its making money was not considered germane, and a series of Silver Grille managers continued to operate the restaurant with their only concerns being high quality service and excellent food.

The pressure of the times, however, meant that in the early 1980s that way of operating The Silver Grille was going to have to change. Margaret Halterlein, who managed The Silver Grille until its closing, stated that she had to review the vast number of employees in the kitchen and needed to let some of them go. In part this move was logical as many food items were then purchased in prepared form rather than having to be prepared entirely on site, as had been the hallmark of the past. The Silver Grille also adapted its menu to meet the changes in American eating habits, and it was open on Sunday when Higbee's began doing business seven days a week. All of these efforts were aimed at improving the profitability of The Silver Grille.

Between 1980 and 1983 Forest City Enterprises completed purchase of the adjacent Terminal Tower, the Cleveland Union Terminal, and related properties for a new urban shopping, office, and hotel complex. Leadership for this project came from Forest City's Albert Ratner and Ruth Miller, and it was aided by Higbee executives, including Herbert Strawbridge and Robert Broadbent, who saw this vibrant new development as the salvation for the Higbee space. They worked closely with the Forest City principals to assure that the development would go forward.

Then in 1987 The Higbee Company was sold to a joint venture of Dillard's Department Store of Little Rock, Arkansas, and the DeBartolo Development Company of Youngstown, Ohio. The new owners intensely examined the operations of The Higbee Company properties they had acquired, and as a result of that study, Dillard's decided to eliminate food service at its downtown Cleveland store, downsize the store to five floors, reconfigure the former bargain basement store into the new men's store, and convert the upper floors into office space.

Dillard management viewed the Tower City development somewhat differently from the way the former Higbee team had. It calculated that the additional restaurant spaces being developed there would prove to be too much competition for The Silver Grille and Pronto Room and that the new upscale shops in the Avenue would be fierce competition for its own lines of merchandise. And so it came about, that despite pleas from the general public, The Silver Grille and the other store restaurants closed at the end of December 1989.

The Silver Grille as it looked for an Irish Import Fair promotion. *(Richard Karberg collection)*

Even after The Silver Grille closed, the unity of design of the room and its furniture remained in evidence. This is how it looked nearly ten years after its closing. *(Richard Karberg photo)*

The Restoration of The Silver Grille

Happily The Silver Grille and adjoining foyer survived their closing. In 1990 work began on gutting the upper floors of the department store that Dillard's no longer needed for retail. The plan was to prepare them for use as office space. The Silver Grille, however, was spared that fate. It was protected under the Historic Building Tax Credits program given to the Higbee Building. Dillard's/ DeBartolo received the tax credits under the proviso that the exterior, street floor, and historic areas on the tenth floor were not demolished or altered.

Progress on the reworking of the other abandoned floors soon came to a standstill. At the time, the office market in downtown Cleveland was being augmented by the addition of the new space provided by the completion of the Key Tower. Supply was outpacing demand, and so the plans for office space in the Higbee Building were put on hold. It was not until early in 2000 that renewed interest in the Higbee space was shown.

Veterans of Silver Grille service continue to meet monthly. Here in February 2002, Grille historians Judith and Richard Karberg (back row) join (front row, left to right) former staffers: Ann Redovian, Albina Rudd, Angela Mylen, and Ann Zupancic. *(Tim Ryan photo)*

The first floor of the former Higbee/Dillard's downtown store is devoid of merchandise following Dillard's abandoning its operations there. The view, in February 2002, looks toward the Prospect entrance. *(Richard Karberg photo)*

In that year Forest City Enterprises assumed full ownership of the Higbee Building. At the same time, ABR Infocom, a telecommunications company, saw the building's vacated upper floors as ideal for creating a "telecom hotel," a facility to house telecommunication equipment for the burgeoning industry. The large open spaces, the ability of the floors to accept the heavy loads required by large pieces of communication equipment, and the building's location in the center of the city made it an ideal home base for telecommunications firms. James Richardson, vice president of development for Forest City Enterprises, was given responsibility for the redevelopment of the entire Higbee Building, and the decision was made to renovate some of the upper floor space for general use as well.

The Higbee Auditorium, adjacent to The Silver Grille, today shows how the 1990 demolition work left the once popular venue. Forest City Enterprises may decide to restore the room sometime in the future. *(Richard Karberg photo)*

Forest City Enterprises turned to the Cleveland architectural firm GSI to do the preliminary planning for the upper floors and specifically to develop plans for the spaces to house the tele-communications firms themselves. Daniel Sirk was the architect in charge.

Forest City Enterprise's plans for the upper floors of the Higbee Building were then complicated by the Dillard's announcement in October 2001 that it would cease store operations at its Public Square location at the close of business on December 31. The closing brought to an end 70 years of the building's primary use as a department store.

The Dillard decision, while not unexpected, meant that Forest City Enterprises now had the responsibility to search for new uses and new tenants for the store's lower concourse level and floors 1 through 4, as well as for the previously vacant upper floors. In the meantime, however, despite the setback from the Dillard's announcement, planning went on for the redevelopment of the remainder of the building.

Independently from the transformation of floors 6-9 as space for telecom firms, Forest City saw the time as opportune to finalize its plans to restore The Silver Grille. While the adjoining areas of the 10th floor had been gutted as part of the 1990 demolition work, the restaurant space and its adjoining foyer had remained intact to conform to the requirements of the Historic Tax Credit program. Though the restaurant had been periodically redecorated over the years, The Silver Grille's distinctive features had remained largely untouched since its opening in 1931.

In February 2002 The Silver Grille space stands ready for restoration. The banquettes and enclosures added by the team of Raymond Loewey and John Snaith in 1962 have been removed to expedite the work. *(Richard Karberg photo)*

The concept that evolved was to restore and reopen The Silver Grille as a room for special events, a use that has been tested and found workable with another classic eatery, the English Oak Room on the concourse level of Tower City Center. Forest City Enterprises has reserved any decision to open The Silver Grille for regular dining until the final occupancy of the entire Higbee Building has been determined.

Still under consideration by Forest City Enterprises is a plan to restore the space once occupied by the Auditorium, which adjoined the Grille on the 10th floor. It once served as a site for presentations, fashion shows, and other events. At times, meals prepared in The Silver Grille kitchen were served there. A restored auditorium could be used for conferences and meetings.

With the department store closed, it was necessary to provide new access to the 10th floor. The solution was found by reopening one of the former Prospect Avenue entrances to the Higbee store, unused during the Dillard's era, and constructing a passage to a newly created elevator lobby on what had once been the Higbee's men's store level (its Prospect store). The new entrance would serve both The Silver Grille and the telecom center cluster of offices on the upper floors of the Higbee Building. In March 2002, to mark the beginning of a new era for the property, Forest City officially renamed it the Higbee Building. The name appears on the marquee above the entranceway, and affixed next to the entrance is one of the original *The Higbee Company* bronze wall plaques.

A worker is cleaning the famous Silver Grille fountain, restoring it as the focal point of the dining room -- April 2002. *(Richard Karberg photo)*

The new entrance to The Silver Grille proudly bears the Higbee name, returned to the building after an absence of 13 years. *(Richard Karberg photo)*

Inside, at the end of the entrance passage, is the elevator lobby. The elevator cabs themselves were refinished to resemble their interiors when first placed into operation. The trim around the elevators was also fashioned to closely resemble the original. Adding to the feeling, the floor indicator panel inside the elevators recalls for passengers the store departments that once had occupied the various floors. With the restoration complete, once again Clevelanders can take an express elevator to the 10th floor of the Higbee Building, just as had been the case when the restaurant originally opened for business.

Planning for The Silver Grille restoration began in summer 2001, and by September John Williams of Process, the Cleveland design firm hired to oversee the restoration, had submitted a proposal for the project. Williams' background included a wide range of design experience since his graduation from the Kent State University School of Architecture. His work at Tower City featured an interdisciplinary approach. Earlier he had successfully completed the design work for the Century, the new restaurant at the Ritz Carlton Tower City Hotel. Plans for the Century restaurant began with a conceptual design, then creating an image, and finally working on the total environment, including furniture and artwork.

In The Silver Grille project, the design was already in place, but the job required considerable research and investigation so that the restored space would faithfully mirror the original. Much time was spent, for example, on determining the right shade of brown carpeting to replicate what had been present in 1931. Additional effort went into discovering the original paint scheme. Scrapings and other techniques were used to select just the right shade of green. The Provenzale Construction Company was hired as the general contractor for the renovation.

Research also determined that the original ceiling of The Silver Grille had been highlighted in aluminum leaf (but subsequently covered with acoustical tile). The aluminum leaf was of interest since the use of this same material was featured in the ceiling in the main concert hall in Severance Hall. Like The Higbee Building, Severance Hall opened in 1931, a hallmark of modern design.

In order to replicate the original appearance, the Dependable Painting Company, which had applied the aluminum leaf in the Severance Hall restoration, was selected as the painting contractor for The Silver Grille. After the acoustical tiles had been removed and the surface prepared, the contractor sprayed Sheffield aluminum paint to those areas which had been originally done in aluminum leaf. Thus yet another connection between Severance Hall and the Higbee Building was put into place. Even the hanging of draperies at the entranceway to The Silver Grille echoes their use at the large Palladian window and in the niches in the Severance Hall lobby.

An application of aluminum paint to the ceiling and to the decorative elements in The Silver Grille restores them to their original appearance -- March 2002. *(Richard Karberg photo)*

Early on a Sunday morning, a helicopter delivers a chiller to the roof of the Higbee Building, part of The Silver Grille's new cooling system. *(Jim Toman photo)*

Another part of The Silver Grille restoration was the return of the elegant 10th floor ladies' and men's restrooms to their original appearance. The 10th floor elevator lobby was cleaned, and the paneling was restored to its original appearance.

In addition to restoring The Silver Grille, Williams and his firm were responsible for planning a service kitchen to handle the needs of the caterers who would serve the food in The Silver Grille. After the restaurant closed in 1989, the original kitchen was torn out and donated to St. Michael's Hospital (then St. Alexis) in 1990.

The intent in restoring The Silver Grille was to return the room to an era of elegance when eating lunch or dinner in a major downtown department store was an event. The room was intended to echo a period when women were expected to wear hats and gloves and men were attired in smart business suits and hats. It reflected the glamour of the heyday of Broadway and Hollywood stars and starlets. The Silver Grille and its furnishings had been crafted in a style which assured their appeal for years to come.

The restoration of The Silver Grille required solving a number of tactical issues. The room needed a new air conditioning system. This meant the installation not only of duct work within the 10th floor, but also a new chiller and other equipment on the roof of the Higbee Building.

The chiller was too large to be

Lillian Beck, (second from left) who started as a waitress at The Silver Grille in 1936, cuts the ribbon to open the restored room on May 11, 2002. She is joined (left to right) by her daughter Nancy Sergi, who also worked as a waitress in the Grille, and by James Richardson and Allan Krulak of Forest City Enterprises. *(Richard Karberg photo)*

Henry Brownell and Marie Strawbridge, mainstays in the history of The Higbee Company, enjoy opening night at the restored Silver Grille. *(Richard Karberg photo)*

Opening night for the restored Silver Grille was a festive event sponsored by Leadership Cleveland. Here party-goers celebrate the return of the fabled room. *(Richard Karberg photo)*

brought up in an elevator, and even had that been possible, there would still have been no way to take it outside to the rooftop. The only solution was the use of a large freight helicopter, which airlifted the unit from the intersection of Euclid Avenue and Ontario Street, which on the morning of April 14, 2002, was closed off to traffic. The unit arrived at the intersection on a flatbed truck, and at about 7:30 a.m. the helicopter came along and raised the heavily secured unit onto the Higbee Building penthouse roof where it was then later connected to the system. The last piece in the restoration process was then in place.

The satisfying ambiance of The Silver Grille lasted through the dreary days of The Great Depression, the anxieties of the war years, and the stressful 1960s and 1970s, only to go dormant in 1989, a victim of budgetary considerations. But instead of remaining forgotten, this environment has now sprung back to life. It will have a second career in providing an atmosphere of glamour and sophistication and in reviving the memories of an older generation. It seems likely also to captivate the imagination and appreciation of a new generation of Clevelanders.

How welcome it is! Enjoy!

Silver Grille recipes have been preserved in three different forms. Ann Zupancic preserved six volumes of recipes and the cost breakdowns for them in books dated 1938 and 1946. Margaret Halterlein had another set of six smaller volumes with the recipes handwritten and reduced to family -- rather than restaurant-size portions. Both Anne Zupancic and Jim McConnell had many typewritten copies of these recipes again reduced to family-size portions. For this volume we have selected a group of recipes which are reproduced in smaller portions, sometimes modified (as noted) or with ingredients generally available today.

Another intriguing issue involves the ingredients used in many of the early recipes. In a pre-cholesterol-conscious era, it was common to see butter, cream, eggs, beef fat, lard, and similar ingredients liberally listed. And while these ingredients may not find favor with the health-conscious food preparers of today, several recipes including them have been included here for both historic as well as gourmet interest.

Enjoy Your Favorite
Higbee Restaurant

THE HIGBEE COMPANY
Cleveland, Ohio

The Afternoon Tea menu for The Silver Grille from the 1960s. *(Margaret Halterlein collection)*

Baked Chicken Breasts in Sour Cream   (4 servings)

1 cup sour cream
2 tsp. soy sauce
½ tsp. garlic salt
2 Tbsp. lemon juice
1 tsp. celery salt

1 tsp. paprika
dash pepper
2 cups seasoned bread crumbs
4 chicken breasts, 6 oz. each
4 Tbsp. melted butter

Mix together sour cream, soy sauce, garlic salt, lemon juice, celery salt, paprika, and pepper. Dip chicken into mixture, and then roll in the seasoned bread crumbs. Arrange pieces in a lightly greased baking dish. Drizzle with the melted butter, and bake uncovered in a 350-degree oven for 45-60 minutes.

Baked Chicken Loaf   (4-6 servings)

2 cups coarsely chopped chicken
2/3 cup soft bread crumbs
1/3 cup cooked rice
1½ Tbsp. butter
1/3 cup chicken broth

2 Tbsp. chopped pimentos
1/3 tsp. salt
1/3 tsp. paprika
2 well-beaten eggs

Mix the ingredients in the order given above. Put into greased loaf pan 4" by 8" by 4". Bake at 350 degrees for one hour or until loaf is set.
Note: This recipe was served cold, with french fries and a fruit salad. It can also be served warm with chicken cream sauce (See following chicken pot pie recipe) or with mushroom sauce, which follows.

Chicken Pot Pie   (makes 4 servings)

5 cups cream sauce (see recipe below)
3 cups diced or pulled chicken meat
¾ cup fresh or frozen peas

¾ cup fresh or frozen carrots
pie crust dough or puff pastry

Combine all ingredients and put into individual or family style baking dish(es) and cover with your favorite pie crust or puff pastry top. Bake until crust is browned (per your crust directions).

Cream Sauce for Chicken Pot Pie   (makes 4 cups)

1/3 cup butter	2 Tbsp. chicken base
½ cup plus 2 Tbsp. flour	1/8 Tbsp. yellow food coloring
4 cups water	Salt to taste

Combine melted butter and flour over a low heat until it bubbles. Slowly add the water, constantly stirring until the mixture is smooth. Add the remainder of the ingredients, and whip until smooth. (Note: Tester chose not to use yellow food coloring.)

Fresh Mushroom Sauce   (makes 3½ cups)

½ stick margarine	1½ cups hot chicken stock
½ lb. mushrooms, cleaned and sliced	salt to taste
6 Tbsp. flour	dash pepper
1 cup half and half, heated	

Saute mushrooms in margarine. Remove from heat, drain, and set aside. Return mushroom juice and margarine to pot, and heat. Add flour, and cook until bubbly. Add hot cream and chicken stock, a small amount at a time, whisking constantly over medium heat. Bring to a full boil. Return mushrooms to sauce. Check for seasoning.

Shrimp Newburg   (makes 6 servings)

1¼ lbs. medium shrimp, cooked	1 tsp. paprika
6 cups hot cream sauce	½ tsp. salt
3 Tbsp. butter	dash pepper
3 Tbsp. chopped onion	dash cayenne pepper
1 tsp. lemon juice	4 Tbsp. white wine or sherry

Saute onions in butter until transparent; then add paprika, shrimp, and lemon juice. Add cream sauce, (see following recipe) seasonings, and wine.

Cream Sauce for Shrimp Newburg

¾ cup butter or margarine	1½ tsp. salt
¾ cup flour	3/4 tsp. pepper
6 cups hot milk	1 or 2 drops yellow food color (optional)

Melt butter in a sauce pan over low heat; whisk in the flour. Cook about 3 minutes or until bubbly. Slowly add the hot milk, stirring constantly. Bring to a full boil, and add seasonings and color.

Baked Macaroni and Cheese   (serves 4)

½ lb. raw macaroni, cooked according to directions
½ cup flour   1½ tsp. salt
½ lb. grated cheddar or American cheese   ⅛ tsp. pepper
½ cup butter or margarine   4 cups milk, hot

Melt butter or margarine until hot, and add flour, stirring constantly until it comes
to a foam. Add hot milk in small amounts, stirring constantly. Add seasonings.
When mixture comes to a full boil, remove it from the stove, and add the cheese.
Stir until the cheese melts, and then fold in the cooked macaroni. Mix well, and
place in a buttered casserole. Bake in a 350-degree oven for 30 minutes.

Bavarian Pork and Sauerkraut   (makes 6 - 8 servings)

¼ cup butter or margarine   ¼ tsp. pepper
1¼ lbs. pork cubes   4 cups drained sauerkraut
2 Tbsp. onion, chopped   2 Tbsp. brown sugar
¾ tsp. paprika   ¼ cup sour cream
¾ tsp. salt

Brown meat in butter or margarine. Add onion, paprika, salt, and pepper. Cook
until meat is tender. If it gets dry, add a little chicken broth or water. Add brown
sugar and sauerkraut. Cook about 1 hour longer. Just before serving, add the sour
cream, and mix well. (Note: The tester suggests increasing onion to ½ cup,
chopped; this entree tastes better the next day)

Baked Cheese Souffle   (serves 8)

3 cups scalded milk   4 large egg whites, beaten until stiff
4 cups fresh bread crumbs   1 tsp. salt
10 oz. grated American cheese   ¼ tsp. pepper
1 Tbsp. melted butter   ⅓ tsp. dry mustard
4 large well-beaten egg yolks

Place bread crumbs in a large bowl. Add grated cheese, melted butter, and seasonings. Pour scalded milk over the mixture, and stir to blend. Gradually fold in
beaten egg yolks, then the beaten egg whites. Place in a well-buttered 9" by 13"
casserole or 8 oz. custard cups. Bake in a 350-degree oven for 40 minutes until the
top is golden brown. Serve with mushroom sauce (see page 52).

Beef Strogonoff (makes 10 cups)

2½ lbs. beef strips
½ cup margarine
1 large onion, sliced
4 cups hot beef broth
salt, pepper, garlic powder to taste

1 lb. sliced mushrooms
¾ cup flour
1 cup water
½ cup red wine
1 cup sour cream

Cut meat into ½" by 1½" strips. Brown meat in margarine. Add onions. Cook about 1 hour or until meat is tender. Add hot broth, seasonings, and wine. Bring to a boil. Add mushrooms, and cook until the mushrooms are done. Combine flour and water (strain so there are no lumps), and add to the meat mixture. Bring to a full boil and cook about 5 minutes. Remove from heat. and blend in the sour cream.

Tuna A La King (makes 6 servings)

½ cup margarine
½ cup flour
4 cups hot milk
¾ tsp. salt
⅛ tsp. pepper
¼ cup diced pimento

½ cup cooked green pepper strips
½ cup mushrooms sauteed in
 2 to 3 tsp. margarine
2 6-oz. cans tuna fish,
 drained and flaked

Heat margarine, add flour, and cook about 3 minutes. Add hot milk, stirring constantly, and bring to a boil. Add the seasonings. Blend in the rest of the ingredients. Serve with rice, noodles, or pastry biscuit.

Higbee's Championship Chili (serves 6-8)

2 lbs. coarse ground sirloin
1 finely chopped onion
1 clove garlic, minced
1 8 oz. can of tomato sauce
1 11oz. can condensed tomato soup
1 cup water
¼ tsp. cayenne pepper

3 Tbsp. chili powder
1 Tbsp. salt
1 Tbsp. paprika
½ tsp. ground pepper
¼ tsp. ground cumin
¼ cup flour mixed with ½ cup water

Saute meat in large sauce pan. Add onions and garlic; cook until onion is soft. Stir in remaining ingredients except flour and water. Cover and simmer for 1 hour. Remove lid, and allow to simmer until excess moisture evaporates (do not let it get too dry). Add flour mixture, and cook until thickened (about 5-10 minutes).

Asparagus With Cheese Sauce   (for 4-5 crepes)

1 cup milk
¾ cup chablis
½ cup grated cheddar cheese

2 Tbsp. flour
2 Tbsp. butter
Pinch salt

Melt butter, add flour, and stir. Add milk, stirring constantly, and cook until thickened. Add cheese, stir to blend, and add chablis and seasonings. Place 4 cooked asparagus spears in crepe, and roll. Pour 4½ Tbsp. cheese sauce over the filled crepe (see following recipe).

Crepe Batter: (makes 16 crepes)

4 whole eggs
4 egg yolks
1 cup milk

¾ cup flour
Salt to taste

Mix flour, eggs, and egg yolks with a wire whisk. Add milk and salt, and beat until thoroughly blended. Heat a small skillet, and brush with oil. Put in enough batter (1-2 Tbsp.), and tilt pan immediately so that the batter will spread over the entire bottom of the pan. Cook the crepe quickly on both sides.   Repeat the process until all the crepes are cooked, stacking them on a plate as they are finished; cover with a sheet of wax paper to prevent drying out.

Welsh Rarebit   (makes 5 cups)

8 Tbsp. butter or margarine
1 tsp. paprika
9 Tbsp. flour
4 cups hot milk

10 oz. grated sharp cheddar cheese
1½ tsp. Worcestershire sauce
¾ tsp. salt
⅛ tsp. white pepper

Melt butter or margarine until hot, and then add the flour, stirring constantly about 5 minutes or until the mixture bubbles. Pour in the hot milk in small amounts, stirring constantly until the sauce is smooth. Add the Worcestershire sauce and seasonings. Remove from the stove, and stir in the grated cheese, mixing until cheese is melted. Keep hot. Garnish each serving with 7 whole almonds.
(Note: In the 1933 version, beef fat was used in this recipe. The rarebit was served over triangles of thinly sliced, toasted white bread.)

Quiche Lorraine (makes 1 quiche)

1 partially baked pie crust shell (baked 5 minutes in 450-degree oven)

¾ cup crumbled bacon	2 cups half and half
1 cup shredded Swiss cheese	½ tsp. salt
4 eggs	¼ tsp. sugar
1 tsp. chopped onion	⅛ tsp. black pepper

Sprinkle bacon, cheese, and onion into baked pie shell. Beat eggs lightly, and then beat in remaining ingredients. Pour cream mixture into the pie shell. Bake pie in a 350-degree oven for 30 minutes or until knife inserted comes out clean. (Note: Tester used an unbaked pie shell and increased baking time slightly. A variation would omit bacon bits, onion, and sugar, and instead substitute ½ tsp. nutmeg and 10 oz. cooked spinach–squeezed in a towel to remove excess water– and baked as above.)

Spaghetti Bake With Tomato and Cheese (makes 6 cups)

4 oz. spaghetti	2½ cups diced tomatoes
4 Tbsp. margarine	1 tsp. salt
1¼ cups chopped onion	4 oz. grated American cheese
1 cup chopped green pepper	⅛ tsp. black pepper

Cook spaghetti in boiling water until tender. Drain. Saute onions, green pepper, and tomatoes until vegetables are tender — about 30 minutes. Add the cooked spaghetti, cheese, and seasonings, and mix well. Place in a 350-degree oven about 30 minutes or until bubbly. If mixture seems dry, add a little water. (Note: Tester says that while this is not "traditional" spaghetti, it makes a very tasty pasta dish.)

Baked Ham Loaf (serves 4)

¾ lb. ground ham	1 egg
½ lb. ground pork	⅓ cup bread crumbs
½ lb. ground veal	⅓ cup cream sauce (See recipe below)

Combine all of the ingredients and mix well. Place in a greased meat loaf pan. Top with a mixture of:

½ tsp. ground cloves, ½ tsp. dry mustard, and 2⅔ Tbsp. sugar

Bake in a 375-degree oven for 45-60 minutes. Serve with mustard sauce: Combine 1 cup mayonnaise and 2 Tbsp. prepared mustard.

Cream Sauce for Ham Loaf

2 Tbsp. butter or margarine
2 Tbsp. flour
1 cup hot milk

¼ tsp. salt
⅛ tsp. pepper
1 drop yellow food coloring

Melt the butter or margarine in a saucepan over low heat. Blend in the flour, and cook approximately 3 minutes or until bubbly. Slowly add the hot milk, stirring constantly. Bring to a full boil, and add seasonings and food coloring.

Hungarian Stuffed Cabbage Rolls (makes 20 cabbage rolls)

1 lb. ground pork
1 lb. ground beef
2 cups cooked rice
1 tsp. salt
dash pepper

¼ cup milk
1 egg
¼ cup chopped onion
1½ heads cabbage
2 cups stewed tomatoes

Combine the ingredients (except the cabbage and tomatoes) and mix well. Use a number 20 scoop (¼ cup) to place mixture on softened cabbage leaves. Roll them up and place in a baking dish. Cover with stewed tomatoes (or 2 cups of cut-up canned tomatoes). Bake in a 400-degree oven for 1 hour. Make the tomato sauce (see recipe on next page), and pour over the cabbage rolls. Cover with a lid or foil and bake 1 hour longer.

Tomato Sauce for Cabbage Rolls

2 Tbsp. margarine or butter
5 Tbsp. chopped onion
4 Tbsp. flour
2 cups canned tomatoes

Paprika, salt, and pepper to taste
1½ cups cream sauce (see recipe below)
2 qts. shredded cabbage
1 cup sour cream

Saute onions in margarine or butter. Add flour, and cook about 5 minutes. Add tomatoes and seasonings. Add cream sauce and shredded cabbage. Cook until cabbage is almost done. Remove from stove, and add sour cream; mix well. Pour the sauce over the cabbage rolls. Cover and bake in a 400-degree oven for 1 hour.

Cream Sauce for Cabbage Rolls

1½ Tbsp. butter or margarine
1½ cups hot milk

1½ Tbsp. flour

Heat butter or margarine, blend in flour, and cook until foamy. Add hot milk, stirring constantly, and bring to a full boil.

Macaroni and Cheese Souffle (makes 4-6 servings)

1 cup fresh bread crumbs
1⅓ cup scalded milk
½ lb. grated American cheese
3 egg yolks beaten
¼ cup chopped pimento
2 Tbsp. melted butter

1 Tbsp. chopped parsley
1 Tbsp. chopped onion
¼ tsp. salt
3 egg whites beaten stiff
¼ tsp. cream of tartar
1⅓ cups cooked macaroni

Combine soft bread crumbs, grated cheese, butter, and salt. Add scalded milk, and mix. Blend in beaten egg yolks until lemon colored. Add pimento, parsley, onions, and cooked macaroni. Fold in beaten egg whites to which cream of tartar has been added. Place in a buttered casserole dish. Place casserole in a pan of hot water and bake in a 350-degree oven for one hour or until firm.

Seafood Pie (serves 6)

⅓ cup butter or margarine
⅓ cup flour
½ tsp. salt
2 cups liquid made of fish liquor and
   milk, fish stock or diluted cream of
   mushroom soup

2 Tbsp. chopped onion
1 cup frozen carrots, peas, or celery
   (or a combination of these)
1 can (16 ozs.) flaked and drained
   salmon
Pastry for a 1 crust pie.

Melt butter in a large saucepan or skillet. Stir in flour and salt, and blend until smooth. Add liquid gradually, and cook until thickened, stirring constantly. Add onion, vegetables, and salmon. Blend thoroughly. Pour into a well-greased 8- or 9-inch pie plate or 1½ quart casserole dish. Top with the pastry which has been marked with several slits. Bake at 425 degrees about 30 minutes, or until crust is lightly browned and casserole is heated through. Note: If desired, 2 to3 cups halibut, cooked and flaked, may be substituted for the salmon.

Hungarian Veal Balls (makes about 6 servings)

1½ lbs. ground veal
dash garlic powder
2½ Tbsp. chopped parsley
1 tsp. salt

dash pepper
5 Tbsp. milk
2 eggs
10 Tbsp. bread crumbs

Combine all ingredients, and mix well. Shape meat into size of small walnuts (about 32 balls), and place into baking pan. Bake in 325-degree oven for about 30 minutes. Drain off liquid. Make sauce (see recipe below), and pour over the balls. Then bake 30 minutes longer. Serve with buttered egg noodles or small dumplings.

Sour Cream Sauce for Veal Balls

6 Tbsp. margarine
1 Tbsp. chopped onion
1/8 tsp. paprika
1/4 cup flour

1½ cups, chicken broth, heated
½ cup sour cream
salt to taste
pepper to taste

Saute onions in margarine with paprika, until they are tender. Add flour, and cook about 3 minutes. Add hot chicken broth, and bring to a boil. Taste for seasonings, and add salt and pepper as desired. Remove from eat, add sour cream, and pour over the veal balls.
Hint: If desired, make twice the amount of sauce, so there is plenty for the noodles or dumplings.

Higbee Special Sandwich

1 square dark rye bread
1 oz. turkey breast slice
1 oz. Swiss cheese slice
1 oz. Canadian bacon slice
1/4 cup Thousand Island dressing

iceberg lettuce
1 slice tomato
1 slice hard-boiled egg
1 pitted black olive
1 slice cooked bacon

Butter the bread on one side, and place buttered side up on a serving dish. Place on the bread the turkey slice, a small leaf of lettuce, the cheese, another leaf of lettuce, and then the Canadian bacon, all in a stack. Cover with a large outer leaf of lettuce, making a dome over the sandwich. Pour the dressing over the dome. On a toothpick, spear the tomato, egg, and black olive, and use to garnish the very top of the dome. Serve with the bacon slice on the side.

The Silver Grille

Special Luncheons

LUNCHEON 75c

Iced Apple Juice, Iced Tomato Juice or Cape Cod Clam Chowder

•

Broiled Whitefish with Mashed Potatoes and
Lettuce with Tartare Dressing

or

Creamed Eggs and Fresh Mushrooms on Dutch Rusk with a Grilled Tomato

or

Scalloped Potatoes with Broiled Bacon, Glazed Apple Sections
and Mixed Vegetables

or

Plate of Fresh Vegetables with Corn Fritters and a Salad

•

Corn Muffins

•

Lemon Chiffon Pie   Marshmallow Frosted Angel Food Cake
Banana Macaroon Float   Fresh Fruit Sundae
Baked Apple with Cream

•

Coffee or Tea

Today's Salad Luncheon 75c

Cantaloupe Ring with Diced Fresh Fruit Salad

or

Stuffed Egg Salad with Hearts of Lettuce, Russian Dressing
and Sliced Tomatoes

•

Assorted Sandwiches or Hard Rolls

•

Lemon Chiffon Pie or Marshmallow Frosted Angel Food Cake

•

Coffee or Tea

LUNCHEON 65c
Spaghetti al'Italienne with
Meat Balls and a
Fresh Fruit Salad
Pot of Coffee

•

with Appetizer 75

•

*with Dessert 75
*with Appetizer and Dessert 85

LUNCHEON 55c
Choice of Dessert or Appetizer

•

Potato and Egg Salad
with Tomato Sections
Corn Muffins

•

Ball of Sherbet, Sliced Oranges
or Stewed Apricots

•

Hot Coffee or Tea

SPECIAL ENTREES
*Beverage 10c Additional

•

Orange Omelette with French Fried Potatoes	60
Scrambled Eggs with Fresh Mushrooms, Fresh Vegetable, Sliced Tomatoes	60
Welsh Rarebit on Melba Toast with Almonds and a Fresh Fruit Salad	60
Corn Muffins Served with Above Entrees	
Bowl of Soup with Toasted Cheese Sandwich, Sliced Tomatoes, Fresh Fruit Sections	50
Iced Fresh Fruit Juice, Ramekin of Asparagus au Gratin, Sliced Tomato and French Toast	60

Friday, August 24th., 1945

All prices are our ceiling prices or below. The ceiling is based on prices charged by us from April 4 to 10, 1943. Our menus or price lists for that week are here for your inspection

A La Carte

•

SOUPS AND RELISHES
Cape Cod Clam Chowder 10-20

Special Relish 10   Orange Juice 15

Celery Hearts 10   Cole Slaw 15

Ripe or Green Olives 10   Iced Tomato Juice 15

SPECIAL SALADS
A Higbee Mixed Salad: (Lettuce, Avocado Pear,
Celery, Sliced Egg, Anchovy with
Roquefort Cheese Dressing) 65

Tossed Raw Vegetable Salad
with Mexican Dressing 55

A Fresh Fruit Salad 55; with Special Dressing 60

Hearts of Lettuce with (Thousand Island, Russian or
Roquefort Cheese Dressing) 45

Corn Muffins or Ry Krisp Served with Above Salads

SANDWICHES
Sliced Hard Boiled Eggs and Lettuce
with 1,000 Island Dressing 35

Ripe Olive, Pimento and Chopped Pecans 30

Chopped Egg, Green Pepper on Whole Wheat 30

Peanut Butter and Jelly 30

Lettuce and Tomato on White 30

Fish Salad Sandwich on Toast 45

American Cheese on Whole Wheat, Ripe Olives 30

Sandwiches on Toast 05c Extra

DESSERTS AND CHILLED SWEETS
*Lemon Chiffon Pie 20
*Marshmallow Frosted Angel Food Cake 20
*Banana Macaroon Float 20
*Fresh Fruit Sundae 20
*Baked Apple with Cream 20
Apple Pie 20
Butterscotch or Chocolate Sundae 20; with Nuts 25

•

BEVERAGES
Iced Tea 10
Fresh Fruit Lemonade 20 Chocolate Malted Milk 25
Coca Cola 10 Bottle of Milk 10 Hires Root Beer 10
Higbee's Coffee, *Cup 10; Pot 15   Postum, Pot 15
*Pot of Tea 10   Orange Pekoe or Mixed Tea

A Silver Grille luncheon menu for August 24, 1945, points out the adherence to war time pricing controls. *(Jim McConnell collection)*

Shoppers' Specials

CREAMED CHICKEN and FRESH VEGETABLES
over Hot Biscuit with a Salad of Summer Fruits

OR

CASSEROLE of CREOLE BEEF and MACARONI
with Fresh Peach and Cream Cheese Salad

Hot Muffins or Clover Leaf Rolls

Choice of a Dessert and Beverage

— **$1.30** —

A La Carte Suggestions

Chilled Tomato Juice 15-25   Chilled Orange Juice 20-35
Fresh Fruit Cup 20
Chicken Broth with Rice 15-25

☆ ☆ ☆

ROAST PRIME RIBS of BEEF with Mustard Pickle,
Hashed Brown Potatoes and a Tossed Salad ... 1.65

SMALL SIRLOIN STEAK with Baked Potato,
Crisp Head Lettuce with Roquefort Dressing 1.65

ROAST HALF SPRING CHICKEN with Whipped Potatoes
and a Fresh Fruit Salad ... 1.50

FRIED HAM STEAK with Pineapple Fritter,
Buttered Fresh Cauliflower 1.25

BROILED NEW ZEALAND LOBSTER, Drawn Butter,
French Fried Potatoes, Tossed Green Salad 1.45

SAUTEED CHICKEN LIVERS with French Fried Onion Rings,
Buttered Green Beans and Broiled Tomato 1.25

WELSH RAREBIT on Melba Toast, Toasted Almonds
and a Fresh Fruit Salad 95

FRIED DEEP SEA SCALLOPS, Tartar Sauce,
French Fried Potatoes, Green Beans and a Salad 1.25

Choice of Hot Muffins or Clover Leaf Rolls

CHOPPED BEEF STEAK on Bun with Lettuce and Tomato,
French Fried Potatoes 85

Beverages

A Pot of Coffee 20   A Bottle of Milk or Buttermilk 15
Iced Lemonade 20   Coca-Cola or Root Beer 20
Iced Tea 20   Instant Sanka or Postum 20
Pot of Tea (Orange Pekoe or Green) 15
Chocolate Malted Milk Shake 35

Monday, August 31, 1959

the Silver Grille

Sandwiches & Salad Plates

Cup of Soup with Warm Shaved
Corned Beef Sandwich on Rye Bread
with Potato and Egg Salad ... 95

Open Hot Sliced White Meat of Turkey
Sandwich with Cream Gravy and
Spiced Apple Ring on White .. 1.00

Club Sandwich 1.25

Sliced Baked Ham and Swiss Cheese
Sandwich on Rye Bread with
Red Pepper Relish 85

Double Deck Minced Chicken Salad
Sandwich and Sliced Tomato
on White Bread, Potato Chips .. 90

Higbee Special Sandwich (Swiss Cheese,
Canadian Bacon, White Meat of
Turkey, Russian Dressing and
Garnish of Tomato with
Sliced Egg) 90

A Bowl of Tossed Greens Salad with
Julienne Ham and Swiss Cheese,
Russian Dressing 95

Ripe Fresh Peach Filled with Cream
Cheese and Nuts, Glace Dressing 75

A Higbee Mixed Salad (Lettuce, Tomato,
Avocado Pear, Celery, Sliced Egg,
Anchovy, Russian Dressing) ... 95

A Salad Bowl of Fresh Fruit Sections
with Glace Dressing 80
with Pineapple Dressing 85
with Creamed Cottage Cheese ... 95

Desserts

Lemon Chiffon Pie, Whipped Cream 20
Apple Pie 20
Mocha Torte 20
Fresh Peach and Almond Float ... 20
Vanilla, Peppermint Stick, Mint,
Chocolate or Coffee Ice Cream ... 20
Imperial Cheddar Cheese with
Toasted Crackers 20
Red Raspberry, Orange or Pineapple
Sherbet 20
Cup of Diced Fresh Fruits 20
Fruit Jello with Whipped Cream 20
Marshmallow, Butterscotch, Chocolate,
Nesselro or Pineapple Sundae ... 25

Served from 4:00 — 7:15 P. M.

THE SILVER GRILLE • THE LOUNGE • THE AUDITORIUM • THE CONFERENCE ROOMS ARE AVAILABLE FOR LUNCHEONS, TEAS, PARTIES.

The Silver Grille luncheon menu for August 31, 1959. *(Margaret Halterlein collection)*

Children's Menu

Polly, put the kettle on,
Polly, put the kettle on,
Polly, put the kettle on,
We'll all have tea.

Little Miss Muffet
Sat on a tuffet,
Eating her curds
and whey;
Along came a spider
and sat down
beside her,
And frightened
Miss Muffet away

The Queen of Hearts,
She made some tarts,
All on a summer's day.
The Knave of Hearts,
He stole the tarts,
And took them
clean away.

Little Jack Horner
Sat in a corner
eating his Christmas
pie;
He put in his thumb,
and he pulled out a plum,
and said, "What a
good boy am I!"

Simple Simon met a pieman
going to the fair;
Said Simple Simon to the pieman,
"Let me taste your ware."
Said the pieman then to Simon
"Show me first your penny."
Said Simple Simon to the pieman,
"Indeed, I have not any!"

CHILDREN'S PARTY LUNCHEON
85¢
SERVED ON SPECIAL LITTLE DISHES

First you set your table from the little sideboard,
then you eat:—

Creamed Chicken, Mashed Potatoes
Fresh Peas and Carrots

A Teeny Tiny Whole Loaf of Bread with Butter

A Pot of Cool Cocoa
and for Dessert,

An ice Cream Cake
with Three Candles

One for You, One for Me,
and One for All the
Other Little Children
in the World

The Silver Grille children's menu illustrated the buffets used to contain the special children's party luncheon of, what else but, creamed chicken–c. 1950. *(Margaret Halterlein collection)*

Children's Party Luncheon 85c

SERVED ON SPECIAL LITTLE DISHES

First you set your Table from the Little Sideboard,

Then You eat:—

Creamed Chicken, Mashed Potatoes
Fresh Peas and Carrots

☆ ☆ ☆

A Teeny Tiny Whole Loaf of Bread with Butter

☆ ☆ ☆

A Pot of Cool Cocoa

and for Dessert,

An Ice Cream Cake
with Three Candles

One for You, One for Me,
and One for All the
Other Little Children
in the World

BEEFBURGER on Toasted Bun with Ketchup
and Potato Chips 55

TEENY TINY WIENERS on Baby Buns 40

CRISP BACON and POACHED EGG on Buttered Toast . . 45

PLATE of MASHED POTATOES and GRAVY,
BUTTERED CARROT ROUNDS and NEW PEAS,
Roll and Butter 45

LITTLE HEN CHICKEN PIE with Mashed Potatoes
and a Vegetable, Roll and Butter 50

CHICKEN SALAD SANDWICH TRIANGLES 45

CHOPPED EGG SANDWICH on Rye Bread 30

PEANUT BUTTER and JELLY SANDWICH 30

BAKED HAM SANDWICH 40

TUNAFISH SALAD SANDWICH TRIANGLES 45

~~~~~~

Cup of Soup 15   Tomato Juice 15

Bottle of White or Chocolate Milk 15

Vanilla or Chocolate Ice Cream . . . 15   Fruit Jello . . . 20

Chocolate Sundae . . . 20   Chocolate Milk Shake . . . 35

The Silver Grille children's menu from the 1960s. *(Margaret Halterlein collection)*

The Higbee Lounge on the 10th floor, designed by Philip Small, was pressed into service to accommodate Christmas season lunch crowds as seen in its transformation into the Winter Garden. *(Ann Zupancic photo)*

Soups and Side Dishes

Cream of Fresh Pea Soup (6 servings)

¹/₃ cup margarine
3 Tbsp. finely chopped onion
½ cup flour
2²/₃ cups hot chicken broth
2 cups hot milk

²/₃ cup hot half and half
2 cups finely chopped cooked peas
Pepper to taste
Salt to taste

Sauté onions in margarine until soft. Add flour and cook until foamy - about 5 minutes. Add hot chicken broth, milk, and cream in small amounts at a time, and bring to a full boil. Add the chopped peas and seasonings to taste.

Cape Cod Chowder   (makes 7 cups)

2 cups diced potatoes
2 Tbsp. margarine
1 cup chopped onion
2 8-oz. bottles of clam juice

2 6- or 8-oz. cans of chopped clams
2 cups hot milk
½ tsp. crushed thyme
Salt and pepper to taste

Peel and dice potatoes. Place in a 3-qt. sauce pot, and cover with water until potatoes are tender. Drain. Meanwhile saute the onions in the margarine until soft. Add the clam juice and milk, and bring to a boil. Add the potatoes and clams. Bring to a boil, and add the seasonings.

Russian Borscht Soup   (makes 4 ½ cups)

¼ cup butter or margarine
¼ cup chopped onion
¼ cup flour
1 1-lb. can of beets grated (keep the juice)
Beet juice (add water to make 1 cup)
1 can chicken broth, heated

1 cup hot half and half
1 tsp. salt
Pinch pepper
Pinch ground cloves
1 tsp. white vinegar
Sour cream for garnish

Saute onions in butter until tender, add the flour, and cook about 3 minutes. Add the hot broth, juice, and cream, stirring constantly until it comes to a full boil. Add the seasonings and vinegar, and mix well. Add the grated beets. Garnish with sour cream.

Canadian Cheese Soup (makes 8 cups)

1 qt. chicken broth
½ cup diced carrots
½ cup diced celery
1 qt. milk
¼ cup butter
½ cup chopped onion
¼ cup flour

4½ tsp. cornstarch
Pinch baking soda
¼ tsp. paprika
Pinch salt
1 cup grated cheddar cheese
1 Tbsp. chopped parsley

Saute onions in butter; then add flour, cornstarch, soda, paprika, and salt. Blend, and cook well. Add hot milk. Cook celery and carrots in stock. When tender, add stock to cream sauce. Add chopped parsley and cheddar cheese, and heat until cheese is melted and blended.

Au Gratin Potatoes   (makes 7 cups)

5 cups cooked and diced potatoes
6 Tbsp. margarine
6 Tbsp. flour
3 cups hot milk

1 tsp. salt
⅛ tsp. pepper
¼ lb. grated cheddar cheese

Melt margarine until hot; then add flour, stirring constantly about 3 minutes. Add milk in small amounts at a time, stirring constantly. Add seasonings, and bring to a full boil. Remove from heat, add the grated cheese, and blend thoroughly. Gently fold in the cooked potatoes. Mix well.Pour into a 4-qt. greased casserole. Bake in a 325-degree oven about 45 minutes or until bubbly. During the last 5 minutes you may add more cheese on top.

Swiss Rice   (makes about 4 cups)

½ cup finely chopped onion
¼ cup finely chopped green pepper
3 Tbsp. butter or margarine
1 1-lb. can of tomatoes

1 tsp. salt
⅛ tsp. pepper
3 cups cooked rice
4 oz. (1 cup) shredded Swiss cheese

In a large skillet sauté and stir onions and green pepper in butter until the onions are tender. Stir in tomatoes, salt, pepper, and cooked rice. Simmer uncovered over low heat about 15 minutes until flavors are blended and the mixture is hot. Stir in Swiss cheese until well blended. Serve hot.

Scalloped Tomatoes (serves 6)

1 chopped onion
4 Tbsp. butter or margarine
2 slices bread, cubed
¼ cup brown sugar

4 cups fresh tomatoes, cut up
½ tsp. salt
¼ tsp. pepper

Sauté onion in butter, add bread cubes, and brown sugar. Stir over low heat 3 to 5 minutes. Stir in tomatoes, and add seasonings. Pour mixture into greased 1½ qt. casserole. Bake in a 350-degree oven 30 minutes.

Corn Oysters (serves 4)

2 cups corn, scraped from the cob (or frozen corn, thawed)
2 well-beaten eggs
¼ cup flour

¼ tsp. baking powder
Salt and pepper to taste

Mix together all ingredients and drop by teaspoon onto hot and greased griddle. Turn once when brown, brown second side, and serve.

Deviled Cheese Ball (makes 1 1⅓ lb. ball)

1 lb. grated Cheddar cheese
2 Tbsp. catsup
1 tsp. Worcestshire sauce
½ tsp. paprika

2 Tbsp. margarine
½ tsp. salt
3 ozs. chopped nuts

Combine ingredients (except for the chopped nuts) in an electric mixer in the order given. Beat until smooth and fluffy. Chill.   Then form into a ball, and roll it in the chopped nuts.

Yellow Custard Rice (makes 4 cups)

2 cups cooked rice
2 eggs
2 cups milk
¼ tsp. salt

⅛ tsp. pepper
¾ tsp. butter
1-2 drops yellow food coloring

Combine all ingredients while rice is still hot. Mix well, and place in a buttered casserole which is placed in a pan of hot water. Bake in a 350-degree oven for 2 hours or until a knife inserted in the rice comes out clean.

Top: A group of shoppers have gathered for luncheon in The Silver Grille on August 10, 1944. Did they all eat creamed chicken? *(Cleveland* Press *Collection of the Cleveland State University Archives)*
Below: From the time the Auditorium opened in 1932, The Silver Grille staff provided refreshments for special events such as this Health and Parent Education Association tea on April 7, 1934. *(Cleveland* Press *Collection of the Cleveland State University Archives)*

Starting in 1974 The Silver Grille began the tradition of giving children a cardboard stove as a memento of their visit. *(Richard Karberg photo)*

Breads and Muffins

Banana Bread   (makes 4 loaves)

1 cup margarine	½ cup water
4 cups sugar	6 cups flour
8 eggs	3 cups mashed bananas
4 tsp. baking soda	

Cream shortening and sugar together. Add eggs, and mix well. Dissolve the baking soda in water. Add the flour alternately with the baking soda. Mix well. Add the mashed bananas on slow speed of an electric mixer, mixing well. Divide into 4 well-greased and floured loaf pans. Bake in a 350-degree oven for 1 hour.

Herbed Biscuits

3 cups flour	½ cup shortening
2 tsp. salt	4 Tbsp. fresh minced parsley
4 tsp. baking powder	2 eggs
1 tsp. baking soda	4 Tbsp. fresh minced chives
Egg glaze (1 egg beaten with 1	1½ cups buttermilk
tsp. water and a pinch of salt)	

Place the flour, salt, baking powder, and baking soda in a mixing bowl, and cut in the shortening using 2 knives or a pastry blender. Continue rapidly until fat is broken up into pieces the size of coarse salt. Stir the herbs into the flour mixture. Blend the eggs in a large measuring cup, beat in the butter and milk, and mix rapidly into the flour with a rubber spatula, turning and pressing the ingredients together to form a dough. Scoop the dough out onto a lightly floured work surface, and with the floured heels of your hands rapidly knead the dough to give it enough body so it can be patted or rolled out (the less you work it, the more tender it will be, but it must have enough body to hold its shape softly). Place the dough on a lightly floured work surface. Pat it or roll it rapidly to a thickness of about ½" and into the size of casserole dishes. Place over filled casserole, pressing dough lightly against the sides of casserole. Paint dough with a coating of egg glaze. Bake in a 400-degree oven about 20 minutes. (You can also cut or drop into biscuits.)

Higbee Muffins (makes 2 dozen muffins)

10 Tbsp. shortening

1 cup sugar

2 egg yolks

4 cups flour

1 tsp. salt

2 Tbsp. baking powder

2 cups milk

2 egg whites, beaten stiff

Cream shortening, add sugar and egg yolks, and cream well. Combine flour, salt, and baking powder. Add to shortening mixture, alternating with enough milk only to moisten the batter. Gently fold in beaten egg whites. Divide the batter into well-greased muffin tins. Bake in 400-degree oven for 20 minutes.

Pumpkin Fruit Bread (makes 2 loaves)

2 cups canned pumpkin

2 cups sugar

$2/3$ cup softened margarine

½ cup water

3 eggs

2½ cups flour

2 tsp. baking soda

1 tsp. salt

1 tsp. cinnamon

½ tsp. ground cloves

$2/3$ cup chopped dates or raisins

$2/3$ cup chopped nuts

Blend the first five ingredients, and beat for 1 minute. Then add the dry ingredients, and stir in the raisins and nuts. Pour into two greased loaf pans. Bake in a 325-degree oven for 50-60 minutes. Cool in pan for 5 minutes; then remove from pan and allow to cool completely.

Raisin Scones (makes 12 scones)

4 cups flour

5 tsp. baking powder

2 tsp. salt

1 cup shortening

6 Tbsp. sugar

Combine ingredients, and blend well. Add to the mixture and stir until just moistened:

> 1 cup milk
>
> 2 eggs
>
> 1 cup raisins

Roll dough ½" thick, and cut into triangles or drop by spoon onto baking sheet. Brush with milk, and sprinkle with sugar. Bake on greased cookie sheets in a 400-degree oven for 10-12 minutes.

Orange Bread   (makes 2 small loaves)

1½ cups flour

2 tsp. baking powder

2 Tbsp. grated orange rind

⅓ tsp. salt

½ cup + 1Tbsp. sugar

½ cup milk

1 egg

2½ Tbsp. cream

In a large bowl combine flour, baking powder, salt, and sugar. Sift dry ingredients, and add the orange rind. In another bowl beat the egg lightly with a whisk. Add the milk and cream. Add this mixture to the flour mixture. Fold in gently. Divide into 2 greased loaf pans. Bake in a 325-degree oven for 1 hour.

Spicy Apple Bread   (makes 2 loaves)

¾ cup margarine

1½ cups brown sugar

3 eggs

3 Tbsp. vinegar combined with
    water to make ¾ cup

1½ tsp. vanilla

3 cups flour

1½ tsp. baking soda

1 tsp. salt

1½ tsp. cinnamon

¾ tsp. nutmeg

½ tsp. allspice

¼ tsp. cloves

2 cups chopped apples

1 cup chopped nuts

Cream margarine and sugar. Add eggs, and beat well. Add vinegar-water mixture and vanilla. Blend well. Add dry ingredients, and mix thoroughly. Stir in apples and nuts. Grease two loaf pans, and line with wax paper. Divide the batter evenly between the pans. Bake in a 350-degree oven 45 to 55 minutes.

Honey Corn Muffins   (makes 12 muffins)

1¾ cups flour

1¼ tsp. baking powder

½ tsp. salt

⅓ cup cornmeal

4 Tbsp. shortening

½ cup diced apples

1 egg

1⅓ cup milk

¼ cup honey

Sift flour once and measure. Add baking powder and salt. Sift again. Add cornmeal. Combine egg, milk, honey, and shortening, and add all at once to the flour-cornmeal mixture, stirring only enough to dampen the flour. Fold in apples. Bake in well-greased muffin tin at 400 degrees for 20 minutes or until brown.

Whole Wheat Muffins (makes 1 dozen)

1 egg
¾ cup milk
½ cup vegetable oil
1 cup whole-wheat flour

1 cup white flour
⅓ cup brown sugar
3 tsp. baking powder
1 tsp. salt

Preheat oven to 400 degrees. Grease muffin tins. Beat egg in medium bowl, and then stir in milk and oil. Stir in remaining ingredients all at once, just until the flour is moistened (batter will be lumpy). Divide batter into muffin tins and bake about 20 minutes. Remove immediately from pan.

Cranberry Orange Bread (makes 3 loaves)

½ cup margarine
1½ cup sugar
1 cup brown sugar
2 Tbsp. grated orange rind
4 eggs
1 cup orange juice
4 cups flour

½ cup milk
1 cup chopped nuts
2 cups whole or chopped
    cranberries (if using frozen berries,
    leave whole)
5 tsp. baking powder
1½ tsp. salt

Cream margarine and add granulated sugar and brown sugar; cream well. Add orange rind and eggs; beat well. Combine orange juice and milk mixture. In another bowl combine the nuts, cranberries, flour, baking powder, and salt. Combine all ingredients, and mix until moistened. Pour into 3 greased loaf pans lined with wax paper. Bake in a 350-degree oven for 1 hour. Cool in pans 5-10 minutes and then remove.

Topping:
Juice of 2 oranges
1½ cup sugar

Combine the orange juice and sugar, bring to a boil, and pour on the bread.

This Nativity scene formed part of Higbee's main floor Christmas decor. *(Higbee Company photo, Richard Karberg collection)*

The fountain and fishpond at the center of The Silver Grille is dressed for the last time in Christmas holiday decor—December 1989. *(Richard Karberg photo)*

Desserts

Angel Food Cake   (makes one cake)

1 cup flour
1²/₃ cups egg whites
½ tsp. salt

1¹/₈ tsp. cream of tartar
1½ cups sugar
1 tsp. vanilla

Sift flour 3 or 4 times. Beat egg whites until frothy. Sprinkle salt and cream of tartar over top, and continue beating until egg whites are just stiff enough to form peaks, but not dry. (If egg whites are thick and not watery, 2 Tbsp. of water may be sprinkled over egg whites while adding cream of tartar and salt.) Gradually fold in the sugar, sifting about 2 Tbsp. at a time over the surface. Fold in the flavoring. Gradually fold in the flour, sifting about ¼ cup at a time over the surface. Turn batter into an ungreased tube pan, and bake in a moderately slow oven at 325 degrees about 1 hour. Invert pan until cake is cold, and then remove from pan. Serve with Strawberry Whipped Cream (see below).

Strawberry Whipped Cream   (makes about 2 cups)

1 cup whipping cream
¼ tsp. lemon juice

2 Tbsp. frozen strawberries, thawed

Whip cream and fold in strawberries and lemon juice

Indian Coconut Rice Cake   (makes 1 cake)

1½ cups butter
1 cup sugar
4 egg yolks
¾ cup farina
½ cup sifted flour

1 tsp. baking powder
1½ cups chopped coconut
1 tsp. vanilla
4 beaten egg whites

Cream butter, add sugar, and beat until light and fluffy. Add egg yolks. Sift farina, flour, and baking powder together; then add to butter mixture, and beat again. Add coconut and vanilla; mix well. Beat whites until stiff but not dry, and fold into the mixture. Divide batter into 2 cake pans (9") buttered and floured. Bake in preheated 350-degree oven 20 to 24 minutes. Cool on rack; then frost with fruited marshmallow frosting.

Fruited Marshmallow Frosting   (frosting for 1 two-layer cake)

1 cup sugar
¼ cup water
2 egg whites
¼ tsp. cream of tartar

¼ tsp. vanilla
6 Tbsp. chopped dates
4 Tbsp. chopped candied cherries
4 Tbsp. raisins

Make a syrup of water and sugar. When the syrup reaches 215 degrees on a candy thermometer, start beating the egg whites in a separate bowl, adding the cream of tartar. When the syrup reaches 225 degrees, remove from heat, and in a fine drizzle, add to the beaten egg whites, and continue to beat for approximately 10 minutes, or until heavy and shiny. Add the vanilla. Fold in the dates, cherries, and raisins. Frost the bottom layer, assemble the cake, and frost the top and sides.

Melt Away Chocolate Pie   (makes 8 servings)

Crust :

6 Tbsp. melted margarine
2 cups flaked coconut

Lightly butter a 9" or 8" pie tin. Combine the coconut and melted margarine. Mix thoroughly and press mixture into pie pan around the bottom and sides. Bake in a 325-degree oven approximately 10 minutes just until the crust is lightly brown in color. Cool thoroughly.

Filling :

1 tsp. instant coffee
2 Tbsp. boiling water

8 oz. chocolate mint candy
5 cups whipped topping

In a small saucepan, dissolve the coffee powder in water, and add chocolate candy (for example, Andes Mints or York Peppermint Patties). Stir the chocolate mixture over low heat until melted. Cool. Fold in the whipped topping and pile into the coconut crust. Freeze several hours or overnight (it will not freeze solid). Cut pie into 8 servings. Garnish with a large dollop of whipped cream in the center of the pie; then grate some of the chocolate candy and sprinkle on top of the whipped cream.

Hot Pecan Sauce for Praline Ice Cream   (makes 2 cups)

½ cup margarine
1 cup firmly packed brown sugar
½ cup granulated sugar

¼ cup milk
½ cup toasted pecan pieces

In a saucepan melt margarine, and stir in brown sugar, granulated sugar, and milk; stir constantly over medium heat until sugar is dissolved. Stir in pecans.

Bread Pudding   (makes 6 servings)

3 cups milk   ¼ tsp. salt
4 Tbsp. margarine   1 tsp. cinnamon
2 eggs   3 cups soft bread cubes
½ cup sugar   ½ cup raisins

Heat oven to 350 degrees. Scald milk, and add margarine. Beat eggs slightly in bowl; then stir in milk mixture, sugar, salt, and cinnamon. Put bread cubes and raisins in a 1½-qt. buttered baking dish. Pour milk mixture over the bread cubes, and stir gently. Place dish in a pan of hot water. Bake 40 to 45 minutes or until a thin-bladed knife inserted 1" from the center comes out clean. Serve warm or cold with cream or whipped cream.

Molasses Crinkle Cookies   (makes 2 ½ dozen)

¾ cup margarine   2 tsp. baking soda
1 cup brown sugar   ¼ tsp. salt
1 egg   ½ tsp. cloves
¼ cup molasses   1 tsp. cinnamon
2¼ cups flour   ½ Tbsp. ginger

Mix all wet ingredients well, add the dry ingredients, and stir well. Scoop into balls, roll in sugar, and place on cookie sheet. Bake in 375-degree oven 10 minutes.

Fudge Upside Down Cake   (makes 8 servings)

Sift together:

      1 cup flour   ¾ cup sugar
      ¼ tsp. salt   2 tsp. baking powder

Add:

      ½ cup of milk
      2 Tbsp. melted butter   1 tsp. vanilla
      1 oz. melted chocolate   ½ cup chopped nuts

Mix all of the above, and pour into a buttered 8" by 8" by 2" pan. Top with a mixture of:

      ½ cup granulated sugar   ½ cup brown sugar
      3 Tbsp. cocoa

Pour 1 cup of hot water over it all. Bake 40 minutes in a 325-degree oven.

Old Fashioned Raisin Bars (makes 4 dozen bars)

1 cup strong coffee
1 cup raisins
1 cup sugar
½ cup salad oil
1 beaten egg
1¾ cups flour

1 tsp. baking soda
½ tsp. cinnamon
½ tsp. nutmeg
¼ tsp. salt
¼ tsp. allspice
⅛ tsp. cloves

Pour hot coffee over the raisins. Cool to lukewarm. Stir in sugar, oil, and egg.
Stir together flour, soda, cinnamon, nutmeg, salt, allspice, and cloves; add raisin
mixture, and stir until combined. Pour into a greased 9" by 13" pan. Bake in a
375-degree oven for 12 to 15 minutes or until done. Cool. Spread with coffee
icing (see recipe below), and sprinkle with ½ cup of nuts if desired.

Coffee Icing

3 Tbsp. margarine
2 cups powdered sugar

1 tsp. vanilla
Strong coffee

Cream margarine and sugar together; then add vanilla and enough coffee for
spreading consistency.

Mexican Chocolate Cake

2 cups sifted flour
2 cups sugar
1 tsp. baking soda
1 tsp. salt
1½ tsp. ground cinnamon
½ tsp. baking powder

¾ cup water
¾ cup buttermilk
½ cup shortening
2 eggs
4 oz. melted unsweetened chocolate
1 tsp. vanilla

Sift together flour, sugar, soda, salt, cinnamon, and baking power into a large mixing
bowl. Add water, buttermilk, shortening, eggs, melted chocolate, and vanilla. Blend
30 seconds in a mixer at low speed, scraping sides and bottom of the bowl constantly.
Beat at high speed 3 minutes, scraping the bowl occasionally. Spread batter evenly
in a greased and floured 13" by 9" by 2" pan or two 9" round layer cake pans. Bake
in a 350-degree oven 40 to 45 minutes (for large pan) or 30 to 35 minutes (for layer
pans). Cool pans on a rack. Spread cooled cake with chocolate frosting.

Mexican Chocolate Frosting

½ cup butter or margarine
2 oz. unsweetened chocolate
¼ cup milk

1 lb. sifted powdered sugar
1 tsp. vanilla
½ cup chopped walnuts

Combine butter, chocolate, and milk in sauce pan; heat until bubbles form around the edge of the pan, stirring occasionally. Remove from heat, and add the sifted powdered sugar, vanilla, and chopped nuts. Beat until spreading consistency. If necessary, add 1 to 2 Tbsp. of milk. Spread on cooled chocolate cake.

Chocolate Chocolate Cream Pie (makes one 9" pie)

10 Tbsp. sugar
5 Tbsp. cocoa
3½ Tbsp. cornstarch
⅛ tsp. salt

1½ cups milk
1¼ cups half and half
1 baked 9" pie shell

Mix sugar, cocoa, cornstarch, and salt. Add enough milk to dissolve the ingredients. Scald the rest of the milk and cream, and add to the above mixture. Cook until the mixture thickens. Pour into the baked pie shell. Cool, and top with whipped cream.

Fruit Squares (makes 16 2" x 2" servings)

½ cup butter
½ cup sugar
1 cup cake flour
1 egg

¼ cup diced walnuts
1 20-oz.can cherry filling
powdered sugar

Grease and flour one 8" by 8" by 2" pan. Cream butter, sugar, and eggs. Add flour; then stir in nuts. Spread ¾ of the dough in the pan, pressing down bottom and up the sides and then spread filling over dough. Put the remaining dough in dollops on top of pie filling. Bake in 350-degree oven 45 minutes. Sprinkle powder sugar on top while still warm.

Maple Pecan Bavarian (serves 10)

¼ cup cold water
1 Tbsp. gelatin
1 cup hot maple syrup

2 egg yolks
1½ cups heavy cream, whipped
6 Tbsp. chopped pecans

continued on page 84

Dissolve gelatin in cold water, and add to the hot syrup. Beat egg yolks into the mixture, and mix well. When the mixture begins to set, fold into beaten whipped cream, and finally fold in the chopped nuts. Divide into 10 dessert dishes.

Almond Cream Pudding (serves 6)

2 cups hot milk
4 Tbsp. farina
1 egg, separated and beaten
6 Tbsp. sugar

¼ tsp. vanilla extract
¼ tsp. almond extract
Pinch   salt

Mix sugar and farina together. Add a small amount of the hot milk to dissolve the mixture, and then fold in the beaten egg yolk and flavorings. Add the rest of the milk. Cook until the mixture thickens, and then add flavorings. Cool until the pan is warm to the touch. Fold in beaten egg whites. Pour into one serving dish, or into individual dishes. Refrigerate.

Cheese Dream Pie

1 Tbsp. gelatin
¼ cup cold water
1 lb. creamed cottage cheese
2 egg yolks, beaten until thick and
   yellow colored
6 Tbsp. sugar

$^1/_3$ cup hot milk
$^1/_3$ cup cold milk
2 egg whites, beaten stiff
6 Tbsp. sugar
1 cup whipping cream
1 tsp. vanilla

Combine gelatin and cold water and set aside. In a mixing bowl whip the cottage cheese. In another pan whip the egg yolks and sugar. Add the hot milk, and cook over hot water until the spoon is coated. Remove from stove, add the gelatin mixture, and stir. Add the cold milk. Beat egg whites stiff, and add the second amount of sugar. Beat the whipping cream stiff. Fold the whipping cream and egg whites into the egg yolks and cheese mixture all at the same time, and pour into the graham cracker crust (see next recipe).

Graham Cracker Crust   (makes 1 9" pie)

1½ cups crushed graham crackers   ½ cup melted butter
½ cup sugar

Combine ingredients and mix. Then press mixture firmly into a 9-inch pie tin.
Sprinkle lightly with cold water and bake in a 300-degree oven for 8 minutes.
Note: This will make a very full pie. If you have some extra filling, it can be
poured in a serving dish and enjoyed separately.

Scotch Shortbread   (makes 16 cookies)

2 cups flour
2 tsp. baking powder
¼ tsp. salt
1 cup butter
½ cup confectioner's sugar

Sift the first 3 ingredients, and set aside. Make sure the butter is at room temperature. Cream the butter until fluffy, and add the sugar slowly, beating until light.
Stir in the sifted dry ingredients. Mixture will be stiff and may require mixing by
hand. Divide the dough in half, and press each half into the bottom of 9" glass pie
plate. Score the dough into 8 wedges with a sharp knife. You may decorate the
shortbread with the tines of a fork or a small cookie stamp before baking. Then
bake at 350 degrees for 20-25 minutes, watching carefully. Bake until the edges
are just brown. Remove from the oven, and cut through immediately on the score
marks. Let cool completely in pan, and then remove carefully (shortbreads are
fragile).

Wooden buffets, like this one, were once used to serve children's meals in The Silver Grille. *(Richard Karberg photo)*

A souvenir key was given out by Mr. Jingeling (played by Earl Keyes) to children who visited Higbee's each Christmas season from 1983 until 1989. *(Jim McConnell collection)*

Starting in 1984 cardboard Higbee trucks were popular mementos for boys who visited The Silver Grille. *(Richard Karberg photo)*

Appetizers

Soup du Jour   Cup **1.25**   Bowl **1.65**   **Frosted Fruit Cup**   **1.25**

Chamberry Mimosa, Cranberry juice, raspberry sherbet and champagne   **2.75**

Cherry Apple Cider, served in our special Holiday Glass,
you keep the glass   **1.95**

Entrees

HOLIDAY CLASSIC

Roast Breast of Turkey with Dressing

Whipped Potatoes   Country Gravy   Green Snap Peas   Cranberry Sauce

4.95

Pumpkin Pie with Whipped Cream and Beverage

5.95

Breast of Chicken en Croute, a tender boneless chicken breast
filled with mushrooms and onions in a delicate sauce and baked
in a butter puff pastry, complemented with bearnaise sauce.
Served with herb buttered carrots and snap green peas   **7.95**

Crunchy Scrod, delicately baked and served with
broccoli spears and herb buttered carrots   **5.75**

Prime Rib Au Jus, prepared to order and served with
oven brown potatoes and a garden green salad   **10.95**

Chicken Pot Pie, Chunks of chicken breast and garden vegetables
in a rich cream sauce, topped with a flaky crust and served with
a fresh fruit or garden green salad   **4.75**

Welsh Rarebit, a classic cheese sauce sprinkled with toasted whole
almonds, served over melba toast with a fresh fruit or garden green salad   **4.25**

Quiche du Jour, a deep dish flaky crust with a different filling each day,
served with a fresh fruit salad and strawberry dipping sauce or glace dressing   **4.75**

The Higbee Special, our specially selected meal of the day,
accompanied by your choice of a cup of hearty soup
or special dessert and beverage   **Priced Daily**

Maurice Salad, julienne strips of ham, turkey, Swiss cheese and
sweet gherkins tossed with lettuce and our own Maurice dressing   **4.75**

Higbee's Trio Salad, featuring our chunky chicken salad,
Albacore tunafish salad and fresh fruit, served with melba toast   **5.25**

Beverages

**Hawaiian Royal Kona,® Decaffeinated Coffee, Tea,
Flavored Teas, Pepsi, Diet Pepsi, Slice, Iced Tea, Milk**   **.75**

For the Gourmet Coffee Lover   1.50   (2 Cup Service)

International Flavored Coffees, Freshly Ground and Brewed.

Emerald Cream   Cafe L'Orange   Vanilla Colada   Dutch Chocolate
Cafe Cinnamon   Decaffeinated Almond Amaretto

The 1987 Silver Grille Christmas menu featured a special turkey dinner to go along with long-time favorites Maurice Salad and Welsh Rarebit. *(Richard Karberg collection)*

Salads and Dressings

Glace Dressing for Fresh Fruit   (makes about 1 cup)

6 Tbsp. super fine sugar
1 tsp. dry mustard
¼ tsp. salt
3 Tbsp. cider vinegar

1 cup minus 1 Tbsp. salad oil
1½ tsp. paprika
⅛ tsp. onion juice

Combine all dry ingredients, and add vinegar and onion juice. Beat with an electric mixer until sugar is dissolved. Add oil in small amounts at a time beating until thick – the consistency of mayonnaise.

Russian Dressing   (makes about 1 cup)

½ cup mayonnaise
6 Tbsp. chili sauce
2 Tbsp. vinegar
1 Tbsp. Worchestshire sauce

½ tsp. salt
¼ cup chopped pimento
¾ tsp. grated onion
Pinch pepper

Combine all the ingredients, and mix well. Store refrigerated in a covered jar.

Maurice Salad   (1 serving)

1½ cups diced iceberg lettuce
1 oz. julienned cooked ham
1 oz. julienned cooked turkey or chicken

1 oz. julienned Swiss cheese
1 tsp. chopped sweet pickle

Combine all ingredients. Mix with ¼ cup of classic Maurice dressing (see recipe below) and place in a bowl lined with lettuce leaves.

Classic Maurice Dressing   (makes 4 servings)

1 cup mayonnaise
1 hard boiled egg, chopped

2 Tbsp. chopped parsley
1 tsp. vinegar

Combine and mix. Note: The original Maurice Dressing was made with a commercial base not currently available. This recipe was developed by a former Silver Grille employee.

Potato and Egg Salad   (makes 5 cups)

4 cups cooked and diced potatoes
1 cup sliced celery
¼ cup oil and vinegar dressing
½ tsp. chopped onion

1 cup mayonnaise
1 tsp. salt
Dash pepper
2 hard cooked and diced eggs

Dice potatoes while still hot, and marinate in oil and vinegar dressing. Add onions.
When cool, add mayonnaise, celery, salt, and pepper, and gently mix in eggs. Refrigerate until serving time.

Higbee French Dressing   (makes 1½ cups)

¾ cup salad oil
2 Tbsp. olive oil
6 Tbsp. cider vinegar
2 Tbsp. water

2 tsp. sugar
1 tsp. salt
½ tsp. pepper

In a jar combine dry ingredients, and add vinegar and water. Shake to dissolve
sugar, and add the oil and olive oil.   Shake.

Spinach and Apple Salad   (makes 6 cups)

4 cups spinach, cut into small pieces
1 cup peeled, seeded, and diced cucumbers
¼ cup Higbee French dressing (see above recipe), to which is added

1 cup Delicious diced apples
1 tsp. grated onion

4 tsp. vinegar
1 tsp. salt

1 Tbsp. sugar
Pinch pepper

Trim and wash spinach, and cut into small pieces. Dice apples into small cubes.
Peel and seed cucumbers, and dice into small cubes. In a jar combine the rest of
the ingredients, add to the spinach mixture, and toss well.

Tuna and Sea Shell Salad   (makes 3¾ cups)

4 oz. uncooked sea shell macaroni
2 6-oz. cans tuna fish, drained, flaked
¼ cup chopped celery
¼ cup chopped green pepper
¼ cup chopped pimento

1 tsp. grated onion
1½ tsp. vinegar
6 Tbsp. mayonnaise
¾ tsp. salt
Pinch pepper

Cook sea shells according to package directions; then drain, rinse, and cool. Combine the rest of the ingredients, and toss well.

Tomato Blossom With Diced Chicken Salad (serves 6-8)

1½ lbs. cooked chicken, diced into large cubes

2 cups chopped celery

1½ Tbsp. fresh dill weed

½ cup sour cream

1½ cup mayonnaise

1 tsp. salt

½ tsp. pepper

1 per serving: 3 oz. whole tomato, bibb lettuce, and diced lettuce

8 slices cucumber per serving

1 sliced hard boiled egg per serving

1 ripe olive per serving

1 dill weed sprig per serving

Combine first 7 ingredients to make chicken salad. Then for each serving, line an 8" by 1" glass plate with bibb lettuce, and top with chopped lettuce. Place the whole tomato, which has been star cut, in the center of the lettuce. Place ⅛ of the mixture in the center of each tomato. Fan out the sliced cucumbers on the left side of the plate. On the right side fan out the sliced egg. Sprinkle paprika over both. Garnish with an olive and dill weed.

Vinaigrette Dressing

1½ cup olive oil

½ cup white wine

1 tsp. minced garlic

1 cup sliced green onion

¼ cup minced parsley

2 tsp. dried oregano

2 tsp. dried basil

1 tsp. sea salt

¼ tsp. ground pepper

Combine ingredients in a screw top jar and refrigerate. Dressing congeals when refrigerated; bring to room temperature before serving.

Beef, Tomato, and Green Bean Salad (makes 4 small servings)

2 cups shredded iceberg lettuce

1 cup julienne cut roast beef

2 cups celery, sliced

½ tsp. onion, finely chopped

2 cups green beans

1 cup fresh tomato, diced

Cook fresh (or frozen) green beans until tender. Cool to room temperature. Marinate the roast beef in French dressing for 1 hour in the refrigerator. Add to other ingredients and serve immediately.

Marinated Fresh Vegetable Salad   (makes 6 servings)

½ cup lima beans
½ cup carrots
½ cup peas
½ cup celery
½ cup green beans
1 cup fresh tomatoes, diced

½ tsp. salt
¼ tsp. pepper
1 Tbsp. onion, chopped fine
2 cups iceberg lettuce, finely shredded
2 cups cabbage, finely shredded
¼ cup French dressing

Use either fresh or frozen lima beans, peas, carrots, and green beans. If fresh, cook until just tender. If frozen, heat until just tender. Cool cooked vegetables to room temperature. Add to all the other ingredients, and chill.

Italian Dressing (makes 2 cups)

½ cup wine vinegar
½ cup olive oil
1 cup salad oil
½ clove garlic, crushed

¼ tsp. salt
¼ tsp. oregano
¼ tsp. celery salt
¼ tsp. sugar

Mix all the ingredients. Store in refrigerator. Shake before using.

Sweet and Sour Dressing   (makes 1½ cups)

¼ cup vinegar
2½ Tbsp. sugar
¼ tsp. oregano
¼ tsp. basil
¾ tsp. dry mustard

Pinch salt
Dash   garlic powder
1 cup salad oil
¼ cup vinegar

Combine in a mixing bowl first vinegar with sugar, oregano, basil, dry mustard, salt, and garlic powder. Mix well with an electric beater. Beat in oil very gradually, and continue until thick. Pour in second vinegar, and mix until blended.

Cabbage, Carrot, and Apple Salad   (serves 4-6)

2 cups cabbage, shredded
2 cups carrots, shredded
1⅓ cups apples, diced small

¼ cup French dressing
½ Tbsp. sugar
Dash salt
Pinch pepper

Combine cabbage, carrots, and apples in a bowl. Pour dressing over all. Add salt and pepper, and toss well.

Silver Grille

by Jean and Joan Larson
with Ann Rudd and Rita Erne
Originally published in *Higbee News and Views,* January 1958

'Twas the day before Christmas, and all through the Grille
Customers were impatient and ready to kill;
"Where is our waitress?" "Who's waiting on us?"
They panted and raged and raised such a fuss.

Frenchie and Maria were dancing a jig;
Dottie and Lottie were having a cig.
From out of the kitchen there arose such a clatter.
It wasn't Stella and Elsie mixing the batter.

Away to the Pink Room we flew like a flash.
The sight made us drop our trays with a crash.
Throughout, the air was cherry and bright;
'Twas the Christmas spirit made everyone light.

Hostesses, servicewomen, waitresses, too
Were having a ball on Higbee Special Brew.
Helene and Louise had mixed it with care.
Isabel, too, had added her share.

From the fountain they took them a
A few shakes of malt,
And Betty (of all things) had been
Generous with salt.

We set down our trays and joined with the crowd,
When back through the din came a voice clear and loud.
"To the front of the room – back to work, all'"
(The voice had an all too familiar drawl.)

"On Anne, on Jean, on Joan and Rita –
Come Mitzi, come Susan, Rosemary, Anita."
Back to our stations we flew in a flash.
Tore open the drawers – to the guests we did dash.

When what to our wondering eyes did appear
But Irma and Mary J. so jolly and dear.
They said not a word, but went straight to their work
They emptied the room and turned with a jerk—

"Girls we commend you on a job well done—
Take the day off and go have some fun."
The waitresses replied as they ran out of sight
"Merry Christmas to all—May your New Year be bright."

Index of Recipes

Index of Recipes